STUDIES IN INTERNATIONAL SECURITY

*

STUDIES IN INTERNATIONAL SECURITY: 5

THE SPREAD OF NUCLEAR WEAPONS

Leonard Beaton
and
John Maddox

FREDERICK A. PRAEGER

Publisher

NEW YORK

FOR

THE INSTITUTE FOR STRATEGIC STUDIES

LONDON

BOOKS THAT MATTER

Published in the United States of America in 1962
by Frederick A. Praeger, Inc., Publisher
64 University Place, New York 3, N.Y.

Printed in Great Britain

CONTENTS

PART I
BECOMING A NUCLEAR POWER

PART II
NINE LEADING CASES

48558

Part III
THE SPREAD

Acknowledgments

This study has been undertaken for The Institute for Strategic Studies in London, whose aims include the fostering of public discussion of defence and disarmament. Its purpose was to discover the extent to which nuclear weapons are spreading and to do this it was necessary to travel extensively in North America, Europe, the Middle East and Asia. The travel costs were paid under a grant made to the Institute by The Rockefeller Foundation. The Editor of *The Guardian*, Mr. Alastair Hetherington, was most generous in allowing us the time for these trips and paying the incidental costs.

The subject raises the main military, economic and political issues in a large number of countries. We have been given the most generous assistance by senior members of the foreign offices, service ministries and atomic energy authorities of the United States, Britain, France, Canada, the Federal Republic of Germany, India, Sweden, Switzerland and Israel. A number of senior officials in the British Government have been particularly generous with their comments and criticism.

We would like to express our special thanks to Sir John Cockcroft, O.M., Sri Jawaharlal Nehru, Sir Raghavan Pillai, Dr. Omond Solandt, Dr. Axel Tunberger of the *Svenska Dagbladet* and the staff of the *Neue Zürcher Zeitung*. Our views on the potentialities of China were partly formed during an exchange of views in London between The Institute for Strategic Studies and The Institute for Defense Analyses of Washington. Our thanks are also due to the staff of the Institute for Strategic Studies and to members of the RAND Corporation for advice at an early stage in the project. The judgments in the following pages are, of course, entirely our own.

Finally, we must acknowledge our gratitude to Mr. Alastair Buchan, Director of The Institute. He has provided us with criticism and advice and has helped to solve many of the problems of joint authorship. Without him this book could not and would not have been written.

L.B.
J.M.

March, 1962

Introduction

Four governments, the United States, the Soviet Union, Britain and France, have nuclear weapons within their unrestricted control. The purpose of this study is to estimate how far beyond these first four the spread of nuclear weapons is likely to go. Two decades ago, these weapons were still an unrealised conception. Few people had appreciated how even more terrible war might become and how profound an impact this technology would have on governments and peoples. A decade ago there were only two nuclear powers, though Britain was soon to follow suit; then France exploded a device in 1960. At the same time a deepening awareness of the military power of these weapons has been accompanied by a rapid advance of nuclear weapons technology. The major powers are now building and testing weapons of far greater power and variety than those they manufactured in the years immediately after the war.

The possibility that a steadily increasing number of countries would come to own nuclear weapons is now causing universal concern. The desire to stop the spread has been a powerful incentive to coordinated action by the great powers, and was one important reason for the lengthy effort to negotiate an end to nuclear tests. The subject is even more urgent for smaller powers who may find themselves faced with a military threat of an entirely different order or who may be driven to consider acquiring these expensive weapons if countries which are similarly placed are doing the same.

There are no laws of science or politics capable of abstract analysis which offer any guide to what will happen. The laws of physics are everywhere the same so that each nation would have to surmount essentially similar obstacles. These are outlined in some detail in Chapter I. Nations with friends among the major powers might get help from them and the present prospects of sharing are outlined in Chapter II. But each country, working in this framework, will take its decision in the light of a wide variety of considerations of its economic and military position, geography, alliances, internal politics and the strength of adversaries. The case studies in Part II are an attempt to discover the considerations which bear on particular countries at the present time. We have visited all the countries studied except China and have attempted to draw together the considerations which are now before the governments concerned.

It will be seen from these nine studies that a decision to manufacture nuclear weapons does not follow automatically from a recognition of the capacity to surmount the technical obstacles. A number of nations have moral objections to nuclear weapons; all of them want to avoid the expense if this is possible; and almost all are concerned with the dangers that a general spread would bring. The progress of military doctrine among the major powers is also being watched with interest. Nuclear weapons are not solving the military problems of the Soviet Union and the United States and have created as many difficulties for Britain and France as they have removed: these lessons are being observed among the middle powers. As long as this mood prevails, there is no justification for the fatalism which has surrounded the problem of the nuclear spread and which has given it the ironic name of the Nth power problem. N at present appears to be a surprisingly small number.

Just as this study is concerned with particular countries, so it is pertinent only to a particular period—the 1960s. Present thinking gives a guide to what might happen up to about 1975, since decisions take ten years or more to implement fully. But what might happen after that is, of course, beyond prediction at the present time. This study can go no farther than an appreciation through the most direct reporting possible of the situation at present. A period of wars and insecurity in the next ten years combined with a weakening of alliances and the spread of nuclear technology could induce a group of countries to take up the options which they now seem to be obtaining. That is for the future. Those who wish to stop the spread—and they appear to include all the major powers and most of the middle and small powers—must study both sides of the present argument in the important countries. They must fashion a world in which middle powers will be secure and in which prestige no longer attaches to the possession of weapons of mass destruction. The present inhibitions among most of the middle powers are a sign that, consciously or unconsciously, there has already been real progress in this direction. The future is in the hands of governments, great and small, and will not be determined by the working of some inexorable law.

PART I
Becoming a Nuclear Power

Chapter 1

The Technical Problems

THE outward sign which distinguishes a nuclear power from other nations is easily recognisable. Just as the seismic signals from a nuclear test travel all over the world, so does the news and the import of such an event. With some justice nations which carry out a nuclear test explosion for the first time may regard themselves as having been in some sense transformed. But in reality a country's first nuclear explosion is only as formal a mark of its transformation into a nuclear power as is a man's twenty-first birthday celebration of his transformation into an adult. Even the manufacture of nuclear explosives on some substantial scale is not in itself sufficient to ensure enhanced military power, for bombs are of no use without means of delivery. So it is that a nation bent on nuclear power must first decide what military or political objectives it wishes to achieve, and has then to put in hand the industrial work that will provide not only the nuclear explosives and the means of turning these into bombs, but also the delivery systems without which these cannot be used.

Such are the facts of nuclear physics and the complexities of modern warfare that even when nations content themselves with the most modest ambitions for their nuclear power, each of these tasks will require a deliberate and a massive industrial effort. From an industrial point of view, there is not merely one difficulty to be surmounted in the acquisition of nuclear power, but a whole complex of difficulties. So far as the manufacture of the nuclear explosives themselves is concerned, the chances are that the spread of familiarity with nuclear technology will reduce the difficulty as the years go by. In contrast, however, the provision of means of delivery for nuclear weapons is not a once and for all undertaking, but a continuing commitment to a programme of industrial development for new weapons systems, and to the creation of industrial plant with which these systems may be manufactured. For even the most modest of nuclear powers must match its delivery systems against those of potential enemies, and these systems are bound to increase in complexity with the years. A nation which commits itself to the maintenance of nuclear power signs a blank cheque on its future financial and industrial resources.

In this chapter the technical difficulties of manufacturing nuclear explosives and of developing and making means for their delivery are considered separately. The ways in which different countries would set out to surmount these difficulties must naturally be varied. Such things as a plentiful supply of cheap water power may, for instance, determine the pattern of a nation's programme for the manufacture of nuclear explosives. The difficulties arising from the need to manufacture suitable delivery systems will vary with the sophistication of the armed forces of likely enemies, their prospects of acquiring defensive weapons from the major powers and the distance over which the weapons would have to be delivered. Effective and independent nuclear power will be a simpler problem if potential enemies are close or badly equipped. In nuclear power, as in other fields, even modest fish can be kings in small pools.

I

NUCLEAR EXPLOSIVES

For practical purposes there are two kinds of nuclear explosives whose use may be considered by nations attaining nuclear power for the first time. These are a particular isotope of naturally occurring uranium, and a particular isotope of the artificial element called plutonium. The uranium isotope is called uranium-235, and natural uranium contains 0.72 per cent of it. This means that one hundredweight of uranium (which is so dense that it would fit into a volume of just over two pints) contains some 12 ounces of the explosive component, also known as fissile uranium. The isotope of plutonium which serves as an explosive is called plutonium-239 or, alternatively, fissile plutonium. It has to be made out of uranium in an atomic reactor. For military purposes the method used for making this plutonium must be one which does not produce too much contamination with another isotope of plutonium called plutonium-240—a circumstance which entails important restrictions on the way in which nuclear reactors for making plutonium can be operated.

Though the explosive properties of fissile uranium and plutonium are very similar, it appears that the small differences in the nuclear properties of the two materials suggest somewhat different uses in the manufacture of weapons. In each case, however, an explosion can only be made to occur if it is arranged that more than a certain critical amount of material is present in a small space. Though the amount of this 'critical mass' varies with the conditions of the explosive and with the purity of the material, it seems that an amount in the neighbourhood of five kilograms of uranium-235 is sufficient to explode spontaneously. This quantity of material would have a volume of roughly half a pint. Still more efficient use may be made of fissile plutonium, though it is likely that great complexity of the detonating mechanism of a bomb is required to ensure that amounts of plutonium smaller than one kilogram will actually explode. For practical purposes and where nations new to the technology of atomic weapons are concerned, it is probably prudent to assume that the amount of plutonium needed to make a rudimentary bomb is not very different from the necessary amount of uranium—that is, five kilograms. It is however more than likely that a nation which resolves on a comprehensive programme of military atomic power, in which would be included tactical, or battlefield, as well as strategic, weapons, would feel impelled to put in hand the manufacture of both these types of explosives. It is significant that the United States has apparently been acquiring plutonium from the United Kingdom even though the amounts of fissile uranium available in North America are far greater than can be needed for the purely military programme.

In theory it is true that certain advantages would result from the use as a military explosive of the fissile material known as 'uranium-233', which would have to be made artificially from thorium in a reactor. In practice, however, a nation would be most likely to manufacture this material by using other fissile materials (such as plutonium) from which bombs could also be made. Thus it is that thorium plays no important part in the early stages of military development programmes. In fact there is no evidence that even the advanced nuclear powers have yet manufactured uranium-233 in usable quantities.

The production of plutonium in atomic reactors is by now a familiar process in many parts of the world, and is as prominent a part of the use of atomic power for peaceful purposes as it is of the technology of atomic weapons. For, except in exceptional circumstances, all atomic reactors which burn uranium as fuel must produce significant amounts of plutonium. In fact, plutonium is formed out of the component of natural uranium which is not fissile in a reactor. In practice nations bent on the attainment of independent nuclear power must be expected to use atomic reactors based on natural uranium metal. Nuclear reactors of this kind were built in the United States during the second world war, and afterwards in the United Kingdom (at Windscale) and in France (at Marcoule). Their characteristic is that something like three-quarters of a pound of fissile plutonium is produced for every pound of uranium-235 consumed in the nuclear reaction. This entails that the rate at which plutonium is produced is proportional to the rate of output of heat energy from the reactor. A reactor producing 1000 kilowatts of heat energy (or one megawatt) will produce plutonium at a rate of about one gram every day. Since plutonium-240 is formed from plutonium-239 inside atomic reactors, and since this is undesirable in the manufacture of weapons, fuel cannot be left beyond a certain time in reactors intended for military production. Because of this restriction it seems that in practice between 300 and 1000 grams of military plutonium can be produced from every tonne (metric ton) of natural uranium. This is merely four or five per cent of the amount of plutonium (adulterated by plutonium-240) which could be obtained from a tonne of uranium in a reactor producing power for electricity generation.

The alternative route to the production of military nuclear explosives involves the separation of the fissile component from natural uranium, and this is carried out in the United

States, the Soviet Union and the United Kingdom by a physical process in which the different components of natural uranium are separated from each other atom by atom. In the process a gaseous chemical made from uranium and fluorine is made to diffuse through the pores of a series of synthetic membranes. This process is called gaseous diffusion. It was chosen as the most economical of several alternative processes investigated in the United States during the war. The material obtained is called enriched uranium because it contains unnaturally great proportions of uranium-235. For making weapons the proportion of this fissile component must be high—sometimes greater than 90 per cent. To countries embarking on the production of nuclear weapons the difficulties of gaseous diffusion stem from the fact that gaseous material containing uranium has to be fed consecutively through some thousands of similar separating units. This entails large capital investment, a large consumption of electricity, and a high standard of construction and operation. The technology of this process is unfamiliar.

Since the process is also radically different from most other kinds of industrial processes, the chance is small that a country without great confidence in its industrial capacity would embark on the construction of a gaseous diffusion plant. From this point of view plutonium is likely to seem a more attractive route to nuclear explosive, and nations are likely to be attracted to nuclear reactors rather than to gaseous diffusion plants as a means of making the essential material. However, in strictly financial terms, there is probably very little to choose between the capital cost of obtaining a specified rate of weapons production by the alternative routes, so that it cannot be assumed that nations will always make their first bombs from reactor plutonium. The attractions of diffusion plants are likely to be especially obvious in nations where cheap electricity is plentifully available, and it was for this reason that the British Government considered the production of fissile uranium in Canada in the early fifties. In the context of schemes for controlling the spread of nuclear weapons technology, it is important to remember that gaseous diffusion plants offer a means by which nations might produce nuclear explosives without having to operate nuclear reactors or to handle substantial amounts of radio-activity whose concealment would be difficult.

More recently prominence has been given to a possible alternative to the diffusion process for separating the fissile isotope from natural uranium. This is the centrifuge method, whose principle is that, in a rapidly rotating cylindrical vessel, the heavier atoms of the non-fissile isotope are relatively concentrated towards the periphery. The use of such devices for separating uranium isotopes was tried in the United States during the war, but not pursued as a practical process because of the correct supposition that it would not be possible to devise centrifuges which could rotate quickly enough so as to yield a worthwhile degree of separation. Since then, however, development in West Germany and in the Netherlands has opened the prospect that economically operating gas centrifuges might be designed to separate fissile uranium with a comparatively modest improvement of up-to-date technology. This is, however, not yet proved. In economic terms the advantages of centrifuges are held to be that the amounts of electricity needed would be roughly a third of those needed in gas diffusion plants and that—according to the sophistication of the centrifuges which can be built—capital costs need not be very much higher than those of diffusion plants designed to yield the same output. But for nations embarking on nuclear power for the first time, the attractiveness of gas centrifuges lies in the possibility that in this way it might be possible to operate on a small scale, and with smaller quantities of uranium metal. It could easily be that the most favourable use of gas centrifuge machines would be in the production of uranium heavily contaminated with uranium-238 but still suitable for weapons.

Though the outcome of the research programmes now under way in several countries cannot be foretold, the likelihood is that it will be several years—perhaps five—before anybody can operate the centrifuge process for producing fissile uranium. Since the more optimistic forecasts of the potentiality of the system depend on the assumption that constructional materials will yield their theoretically best performances, it is likely that some of the claims made for the process will prove to be

unattainable. Moreover it is more than probable that the problem of maintaining such sophisticated machinery as a high
speed gas centrifuge—with moving parts travelling at speeds
up to 1000 miles an hour—are always likely to be severe. So
there can be no certainty at this point that the centrifuge process will provide an easy alternative to more familiar methods
of making nuclear explosives, even for nations to which the
possibility of being able to operate on a small scale is attractive. It is in any case certain that the process cannot have any
significant bearing on the international distribution of military
nuclear power until the late sixties.

The official view of the United States Atomic Energy
Commission (made public by its Chairman, Mr. McCone, in
1960) is even more discouraging. While admitting the theoretical advantages of gas centrifuges, Mr. McCone said that
'even after substantial improvements have been made thousands of gas centrifuges probably would be required to produce
enough enriched uranium for one crude weapon a year. Including auxiliaries a plant of this type might cost several
thousand dollars per centrifuge.' Against this background it
may well be that the international importance of the gas centrifuge process rests entirely on the fact that it presents unfamiliar and considerable difficulties to those who would
devise systems for controlling the production of nuclear explosives by international agreement.

In any case, in technology it is easier to imitate than to
break new ground. Together with the technical difficulty of
making fissile uranium, this is likely to be one of the most
powerful reasons for supposing that countries embarking for
the first time on the production of nuclear explosives will start
by building natural uranium reactors, and will set out to
manufacture fissile plutonium. This assumption is made in the
attempt which follows to analyse the difficulties of manufacturing atomic weapons. Even if some nation should choose the
alternative route, its advantages would not be great, so an
analysis based on nuclear reactors will still be a valid guide to
the technical difficulties.

As well as deciding on the method to be used for making its
rudimentary explosive material, a nation must of course decide

on the scale of plutonium production most likely to satisfy its political or military goals. Virtually any rate of production between a few kilograms a year and several tonnes a year may be considered to be sufficient or necessary in different circumstances. So as to make analysis clearer, it will be assumed that a nation seeking nuclear weapons will aim at one or other of two programmes for plutonium production. The smaller of these might be sufficient to build up a token nuclear force, and consists of the production of some 40 kilograms of plutonium every year. This is roughly half of the rate of production in France in 1959 and 1960. The second programme is for the production of 1000 kilograms (or one tonne) of plutonium every year, and corresponds to a much greater industrial effort. By comparison the total plutonium production from the eight British reactors at Calder Hall and at Chapelcross in Scotland would amount to something like 450 kilograms a year if these installations were operated assiduously.

A further point to be decided—though not necessarily at the outset of a programme for making nuclear explosives—concerns the nature of the weapons to be manufactured. The point here is that the explosive power of a given amount of plutonium may be—in principle at least—enormously enhanced if this is used for making the detonating mechanism for thermonuclear weapons. Nations beginning on the attainment of nuclear power cannot fail to be impressed by the fact that by this means the explosive power of a simple bomb can be increased perhaps a hundred times without any substantial addition to the industrial effort needed. To be sure, there is some evidence that plutonium is not the most suitable explosive for use in thermonuclear wepaons, but in the discussion of the spread of nuclear weapons, the prospect should not be overlooked that nations which acquire nuclear explosives may be able quickly to equip themselves with the most powerful of existing weapons. Nevertheless, not every embryo nuclear power may wish to make thermonuclear weapons. For example a nation bent on making nuclear weapons for use only in tactical situations may remain content with weapons based entirely on fissile material.

In what follows an attempt will be made to distinguish

from each other the difficulties likely to be encountered in mounting a programme for manufacturing plutonium. Though this process has the virtue of suggesting the scale of effort likely to be needed in a military programme, it is perhaps prudent to recall that none of the ways in which countries are likely to find difficulty has the character of a bottleneck in the strictest sense. Great though particular obstacles may appear, none of them in itself suffices to deter a nation from the manufacture of nuclear explosives. Only when they are considered together is the magnitude of the effort needed to mount a military weapons programme likely to seem overwhelming to many aspirant nuclear powers.

Information

The first hurdle to be surmounted in the manufacture of atomic weapons is the gathering of the scientific and technical information necessary to carry out various parts of the work. In spite of the great secrecy which attends the relevant processes in the nations already possessed of atomic weapons, basic information is as freely available as is information about other industrial processes of a novel, complicated and competitive character—the manufacture of polythene for example. In other words it is possible to gather from available sources full information about the methods which are best followed at various stages of the manufacture of atomic weapons. Information about the actual operation of these processes is detailed enough to be able to specify the degree of efficiency which must be aimed at during the various stages of weapons manufacture.

Basic information about the properties of uranium nuclei, for instance, has been public knowledge since the United Nations Conference on Atomic Energy in 1955. Since that time publication in this field has been increasingly detailed. This may be of great importance in the preliminary design of bombs as well as of nuclear reactors. Similarly the principles of different kinds of reactor construction are available in the technical literature, as are important properties of materials which have to be used in building reactors. Information is less freely available about the processes in which uranium discharged from reactors must be processed chemically so as to recover the plutonium formed. Even though the principles on which this work has to be carried out have been known for many years, details of the operation of existing plants which would be of great assistance to potential designers of new plants are not yet public knowledge. It is likely, however, that this situation will be transformed with the development of such projects as that known as 'EUROCHEMIC' in which a consortium of European countries under the aegis of the European Nuclear Energy Agency plans to develop and to operate a plutonium processing plant at Mol in Belgium. In this and the other stages towards the end of the process of manufacturing atomic weapons, there is, of course, a risk that faulty design of plant may make possible premature nuclear reactions leading to serious radiation accidents.

Naturally enough the most serious gaps in publicly available information about nuclear weapons concern the actual design of the weapon itself. However, the principles on which these devices work are now well-known, and it is likely that a properly equipped laboratory could be used to carry through the development programme needed to fashion weapons out of nuclear explosives without much difficulty. There would have to be field trials with different configurations of conventional explosives so as to test out different methods of detonation, and there would have to be measurements of the physical properties of small quantities (less than the critical mass) of nuclear explosive.

The need of development work of this kind would not be confined to the fashioning of explosive material into weapons. On the contrary, a certain amount of research and development work would have to be undertaken with all parts of the programme. For there is an important sense in which basic information about such things as the properties of uranium and of other nuclei is not a sufficient guide to practical design. In the manufacture of plutonium there are, in fact, several points at which experimental investigation is the only certain means of providing guidance for the design of machinery. Thus, for example, impurities in materials destined for use in nuclear reactor construction may have an important influence on the efficiency with which the reactor will operate, and the most accurate means of finding out how great this effect will be is to carry out experiments in which samples of the materials concerned are studied in circumstances similar in many ways to those likely to be encountered in actual operation.

This implies that the ready availability of technical information about the manufacture of nuclear explosives will not enable a nation bent on the production of weapons to dispense with research and development work. Even the most economical effort would seem to require a laboratory employing a hundred or so people and some of the most advanced techniques of science. It is significant that the countries which have already made nuclear weapons have found it prudent to expend much greater efforts on research and development, though of course these nations have usually been concerned with much wider objectives than the simple production of nuclear weapons.

Raw Materials

Of the raw materials needed for a programme to manufacture plutonium, two are conspicuous because they are not needed in tonne quantities in any other kind of industrial activity. Thus obtaining the uranium used as fuel in atomic reactors (for the production of plutonium or electricity or both) must always be a special problem. So is the task of providing the material known as a 'moderator' which is necessary so that the nuclear fission reaction shall sustain itself. Though a variety of materials may fill this function, only graphite (a form of carbon) and heavy water are likely to be used in a new atomic energy programme. Of these materials, heavy water makes possible the design of compact reactors requiring comparatively little uranium as fuel. For military purposes, however, this compactness is not entirely an advantage, for it means that fuel would have to be discharged from the reactor every few days, so that the productivity of the installation is lessened.

Even for small military production programmes, comparatively large quantities of uranium will be needed. Something

between one and three tonnes of the metal are needed to produce one kilogram of military plutonium. This means that
even the smaller of the two production programmes may
require up to 125 tonnes of uranium a year. For the larger
programme, up to 300 tonnes of uranium a year might have to
be found. Enough extra uranium would have to be provided
for an initial charge of uranium, and for the smaller programme this could amount to a whole year's consumption.
(The fuel charge in one Calder Hall reactor, producing 56 kgs.
of plutonium a year, amounts to 127 tonnes).

Where would a nation embarked on a programme of atomic
power for military purposes obtain these quantities of uranium? Even the richest ores contain small proportions of uranium metal so that they are at once expensive and difficult to
work. Pockets of ore sufficiently concentrated in uranium
(and containing perhaps as much as one per cent of the
metal) to be economical foundations for a production programme are rare. Ore bodies sufficient to support a production
of about 100 tonnes a year or more are to be found in a number
of countries, including France, Sweden and West Germany;
but these ore bodies are not rich enough to support a major
production programme. For this purpose supplies would have
to be obtained from one of the major ore deposits now known.
Apart from the orefields in Canada, the United States, the
Union of South Africa and the Katanga province of the Congo,
it is also known that major deposits of uranium ore are to be
found in Eastern Europe, South-eastern Siberia, Sinkiang
province on the Chinese mainland and in Australia.

The production of these major orefields in recent years has
been greater than the demand, principally because the development of civilian atomic power has been slower than had
originally been expected. This situation has not yet made it
easy for nations, without uranium of their own, to satisfy their
needs by buying on a free market, for all the major producing
nations have legislation which has the effect of making uranium production a government monopoly. Ownership of
uranium metal is automatically vested in the government of
the producing nation. This was intended to ensure that the
purchase of substantial supplies of uranium must always

require not merely commercial but also political agreement. So far important quantities of uranium have not been transferred to countries not already possessed of nuclear weapons without some kind of assurance that this will not be used for military purposes, but there is of course no guarantee that this situation will never change. In particular there is some uncertainty about the uses which may in the future be made of uranium deposits in the Congo, South Africa and Brazil. In the Communist bloc it seems that all except the Chinese deposits of uranium ore are closely controlled by the Soviet Union (mainly through the agency of trade agreements), and that in practice uranium is not supplied to satellite countries unless its use is specified, and is not supplied in any substantial quantity to nations outside the Soviet orbit.

Consequently as things stand at present, uranium to supply a really large (100 kg.) plutonium production programme could only be acquired by a nation fortunate enough to have access to substantial supplies. Other nations will have to be content with a smaller scale of production based on domestic ores. It is perhaps worth recalling at this point that the cost even of modest procurement programmes in this field will not be cheap. It is unlikely that the exploitation of small ore bodies could yield uranium at a cost of less than £10,000 a tonne, which implies an annual production cost of more than £1.25 millions for the smaller programme and more than £30 millions for the larger programme.

Supplies of heavy water or of graphite to act as moderators of nuclear reactions are restricted not by physical but by industrial difficulties. Each of them has to be manufactured by a somewhat unusual industrial process. Though some 30 tonnes of heavy water might suffice to make a reactor producing 40 kg. of plutonium a year, the material is expensive to produce independently (perhaps as much as £50,000 a tonne). By contrast graphite is apparently easier to produce, and there would seem no reason why the material should not be bought from a number of production plants in Europe and elsewhere. For a reactor producing 40 kg. of plutonium a year something like 600 tonnes of graphite of special quality and carefully machined shape would have to be produced. This would entail the production of some 1000 tonnes of unshaped graphite. At a Swiss plant an annual productive capacity of this amount (together with a useful amount of graphite for use in the electrical industry) has been obtained by the investment of £1 million. The raw material for graphite production is petroleum, but quantities of chemicals such as fluorine are also needed. The cost of producing the graphite needed to equip a single 40 kg. a year reactor might be half a million pounds. Independent manufacture of the graphite needed for the more substantial scale of production would entail the creation of a very large industrial complex (with a capital cost of perhaps £10 millions).

An important aspect of the programme for obtaining raw materials which would have to be mounted by a nation planning to manufacture nuclear weapons is the need for great purity—in the chemical sense—of the materials used in all parts of reactor construction. This applies to cooling gases and to certain steel components as well as to the moderator, the uranium fuel, and the metal which may be chosen as a container for the latter. These demands are in fact more stringent than in most other branches of conventional industry, and are especially difficult to meet because such comparatively large quantities of materials have to be produced. Merely satisfying these qualitative needs would tax the resources of a nation without a metallurgical industry of some sophistication.

Construction and Operation of Reactors

To build a nuclear reactor is a major constructional activity. However compact the heart of a reactor may be, the great masses of concrete necessary to ensure human safety mean that the complete installation must be physically a large one. In the construction of the reactors at Calder Hall a labour force which reached 2000 men at its peak was deployed for a period of some years. Tens of thousands of tons of concrete had to be poured. Steel had to be welded in circumstances which made the greatest demands on the techniques of steel manipulation. In these reactors and in all others a great complexity of electrical and electronic instrumentation is necessary, and this must certainly imply that only the more sophisticated among industrial nations can hope to provide these installations without making special (and therefore costly) attempts at rapid and unbalanced industrial development. But the problem here is not so much a matter of the availability of certain specialised skills, but of the complexity of the pattern in which these must be deployed. The inhibiting consequences of this consideration can be inferred from recent experiences in the peaceful exploitation of atomic energy, where programmes for the exchange of technical information on nuclear technology have not yet enabled more than a handful of countries to build power producing reactors for themselves. Apart from Canada and Sweden, most nations appear to have found it necessary to seek help from one of the established nuclear powers in the construction of peaceful power stations.

Probably the effort which would have to be expended on the construction of plutonium producing reactors is the most serious obstacle in the execution of a programme of military atomic power. For no amount of cleverness in design can make up for a shortage of the necessary kind of engineering experience and for the lack of industrial facilities for making the specialised equipment needed in reactor construction. For this reason the cost of building plutonium reactors in advanced industrial societies is no guide to the difficulty that would be encountered elsewhere. Though a reactor producing 40 kgs. of plutonium a year might be built in Britain for £8 or £10 million, a similar scheme in a less technically advanced society might entail the spending of several times as much money on new industrial facilities and the industrial training needed to go with them. Though in an advanced nation the industrial investment to provide a single plutonium producing reactor may not be very different from that necessary to build, for example, a modern fertiliser plant, in a nation such as India the same project might involve as much industrial effort as the building of a modern steelworks.

The management of nuclear reactors is also likely to tax the resources of less advanced industrial countries, though this will only be an important consideration where there is no experience even of such comparatively familiar industrial processes as oil refining, steel production or even airline operation. The principal needs are those of discipline and responsible activity by numbers of skilled men. The numbers involved may be small, but the experience of those concerned with international technical assistance of all kinds is that shortages of managerial skills are often the most important hindrances to progress.

It follows from this that only really advanced nations which are also industrially strong will be able to mount the more ambitious type of nuclear production programme. The scale of production sustained over the last few years in the United Kingdom has probably been determined as much by considerations of what could economically be accomplished as by more objective arguments. Moreover the programme which has been in some sense a maximum effort for the United Kingdom might well have been an impossible burden for a nation like China, at least in the last few years. For in spite of the potential economic and industrial strength of the Chinese mainland, the ancillary production facilities needed to embark on a serious amount of nuclear explosives production are—in many respects—entirely lacking. It will be some years before Chinese industrial sophistication has reached the point at which a full-scale programme of military nuclear power could be undertaken without strain.

A further difficulty in a military explosives production programme is the separation of plutonium—the intended product—from the unused uranium and from the highly radio-active material which accumulates within spent fuel. In Britain this process is carried out at a chemical separation plant at Windscale. Similar facilities exist in connection with the military production reactors in the United States and in France, while the Eurochemic plant at Mol will be capable of treating up to 350 kgs. of uranium fuel every day. The development of these facilities is a sophisticated problem in chemical engineering, further complicated by the radio-activity of the materials to be handled (which makes repair and maintenance virtually impossible) and by the dangers that a concentration of plutonium sufficient to cause some kind of a nuclear explosion may occur in parts of the plant. It is not therefore surprising that facilities of this kind are comparatively uncommon. However there is every reason to expect that these processes will become much more familiar in the remainder of this decade, and that countries wishing to retain the option to make atomic weapons will put in hand, at an early stage, a research and development programme to design a chemical separation plant. In this connection it should be remarked that the cost of the Eurochemic development is estimated to be nearly £8 millions. The plant that will result would only be sufficient to process the output from a reactor yielding 40 kgs. of plutonium every year. An Indian pilot project for a plant of this kind is costing nearly £3 millions.

Tests

Information for the design of actual weapons is obtained partly from openly available sources and partly by means of laboratory experiments with samples of the material—plutonium or fissile uranium—actually concerned. On the basis of this work it should be possible to infer with some accuracy what amount of nuclear explosive will have to be assembled so as to yield a nuclear explosion. But estimating the actual yield of this explosion is more difficult, and probable errors of some 20 per cent or so are common in weapons technology. Thus there arises in any weapons programme a point at which the actual testing of a weapon becomes a technical necessity. It could, of course, be argued that an uncertainty of as much as 20 per cent in the yield of a nuclear explosion is not important. There can be few military situations in which a weapon would succeed if its yield were 25,000 tons of TNT equivalent, and fail if the yield were 20 per cent less than this, or the equivalent of 20,000 tons of TNT. But especially in the development of military weapons, seeing is believing. It is hard to believe that a military commander would be content to rely on weapons which had never been tested, however certain it might be on theoretical grounds that they would perform as designed.

In most cases this technical argument in favour of nuclear

tests is likely to be reinforced by political arguments. For nations seeking nuclear power will often calculate that their objectives would not be attained if the possession of bombs were not demonstrated for the benefit of potential rivals or enemies. So it is that the planning and the conduct of a more or less ambitious series of nuclear test explosions is likely to be the culmination of all programmes of explosives production. Two kinds of difficulties are likely to arise in this attempt.

In the first place there are technical difficulties. Not all nations are provided with deserts within their boundaries. Uninhabited oceanic islands are not always accessible. Accordingly it may be difficult for many nations to find places in which bombs could be tested safely without causing harm to people or to other forms of life by their radio-activity. Finding a site in a country even as sparsely inhabited as Sweden appears to be considered—at least by the Swedes—as almost insuperably difficult. Where then would a Swiss bomb, or a German bomb, be tested? In these and other cases the need actually to test atomic weapons would be a serious obstacle in the attainment of nuclear power. To be sure, a shortage of testing sites on the surface of available territory might persuade nations to carry out underground tests instead. But this is a considerable handicap in making accurate assessments of the power of what would be a novel type of physical phenomenon. In any case, the accumulated experience of underground nuclear explosions is not yet adequate to guarantee that they will always be safe. Special techniques are required and even if no damage was caused on the surface, water suppplies might be contaminatcd by radioactivity. Nations might, alternatively, seek to test bombs in space or from a ship in some deserted ocean like the Pacific; but either of these would require elaborate equipment and would bring only a meagre return of information. Testing in space would, of course, need very dependable rockets.

Political considerations—international or domestic—may also make it difficult for some nations to test bombs. Internal opposition to the testing of bombs would probably be important in nations such as Japan. The likelihood of similar public criticism is also frequently mentioned in Sweden.

Though opposition to nuclear testing because of the radio-active fallout which accompanies them has not apparently modified the military policy of nations bent on the acquisition of nuclear weapons, it is probably prudent to keep this possibility in mind. Opposition to testing as such or even the simple lack of a suitable place might persuade some nations to halt their programmes for the production of nuclear weapons at the point at which weapons are being fabricated but have not been tested. In principle at least such an expedient would confer on a nation the capacity to become an active nuclear power very quickly, but would allow it to escape some of the disadvantages which accompany the possession of nuclear weapons.

Manpower and Money

The economic cost of a programme for producing nuclear explosives is bound to be high, whether it is measured by the amount of money spent or by the numbers of men employed. Because the production of a material like plutonium requires the creation of a new industry, this is not surprising. But because of its inherent technical complexity, the economic demands of a nuclear power programme are disproportionately great. To make plutonium a nation must call on the efforts of some of its most skilled men and its most specialised productive facilities. The real cost of doing this cannot adequately be assessed by the recitation of numbers of men and sums of money. It is however true that the production of military nuclear explosives is likely to yield substantial economies of scale. Bomb for bomb, the largest programmes are the cheapest. Research and development plays an important part and the more use which can be made of it, the less will be the true cost of each unit of explosive power.

Money costs are the easiest to estimate. So far as the plant and equipment needed to produce 40 kgs. of plutonium a year is concerned, accurate estimates of cost for some parts of the work are available from the experience of countries like France. It may in this way be inferred that the capital costs of such a programme would amount to something between £25 millions and £30 millions. The annual cost of keeping these plants supplied with fuel and of operating them would probably be between £8 millions and £10 millions. For the larger programme, producing 1000 kgs. of plutonium a year, initial costs should lie between £260 millions and £500 millions. Running costs will depend on the extent to which electricity is generated from the plutonium reactors, and is likely to lie in the region of £15,000 or £20,000 for each kilogram of plutonium produced. These figures are consistent with the statement by Mr. McCone of the U.S. AEC in 1960, that '. . . it is possible for a country to develop a plutonium production capability to produce one crude weapon per year with an investment of the order of 50 million dollars.' The application of plutonium technology, the additional development work and the construction of a small plutonium production complex would not be a simple task. In order to accomplish this within a period of four or five years a country must have substantial technical and industrial capability of its own, or it must receive assistance from a country that has such a capability.

The significance of these figures must vary from country to country. In terms of money alone, however, there can be no industrialised country which could not find the capital investment needed to support the smaller plutonium producing programme. On the other hand the cost of a substantial production programme is very high, and must be an important consideration in the economy of all but the most prosperous countries. To develop facilities on this scale in a reasonably short period of time—say five years—would entail a rate of capital investment in plant and machinery comparable with that spent in Britain each year on new electricity generating stations (conventional as well as nuclear). For a nation like India (or China) the cost would be comparable with that of the largest steelworks (or perhaps two of them) or with the capital cost of the entire electricity generating systems. Such costs are not prohibitively large, but there can be no question that before less advanced nations take them they will most solemnly weigh the arguments in favour of a large plutonium programme against the needs for other kinds of capital investments.

The demands of a nuclear power programme for manpower take two forms. In the first place there is a need for men skilled as machinists and maintenance engineers, metallurgical process workers and steel welders, who can carry out the necessary constructional and operating work. There must be skilled scientists and engineers who can design plant, carry out the development inevitably necessary even in programmes well supplied with outside assistance, and then provide the continuing analysis of operating performance which is an essential means of ensuring safety. The second requirement is probably the most difficult to satisfy, though even in advanced countries certain kinds of technological skill will be scarce. Apart from the force of men needed during the initial construction of plutonium producing plant, it is most probable that a permanent force of some hundreds of technologists would be needed on a full time basis to operate and to service it, and that even the smallest programme for plutonium production would demand a laboratory staffed by close to a hundred professional scientists and engineers. The large plutonium programme (100 kgs. a year) would require upwards of some 10,000 technically skilled workers (some of whom would be qualified technologists) and a permanent research effort supported by some hundreds of scientists. To the extent that these rough estimates may be in error, they will be conservative. Experience in Sweden and in Britain respectively has shown that larger forces of trained men are needed to support both the smaller and the more ambitious plutonium production programmes.

For most countries the economic difficulties of carrying through a plutonium production programme will be made more apparent by the shortage of men than the difficulty of finding the money for building unusual plant and for operating it. It is also significant that many of these difficulties will persist even if substantial assistance with the construction of plutonium producing reactors is provided by other nations. Moreover, it must be expected that numerical shortages of the necessary skilled people will make it impossible for some countries wishing to do so to mount even the smallest nuclear power programme for military purposes. It is not merely that all the

new countries of Africa, most of those in South America and—
with the exception of Israel—all the countries of the Middle
East would be unable to find enough of the right people to
make nuclear explosives; even countries like Spain, Portugal
and Greece in which advanced technologies are largely un-
developed would find the problems of getting the men to make
nuclear weapons insurmountable. By contrast, most of the
industrialised nations of Western Europe would not be prevented from fulfilling ambitions in this field by shortages of people.
To this extent the capacity to make nuclear weapons is as much
a mark of industrial advancement as, for example, the capacity
to make motor cars.

Time

The first programme of nuclear power to be carried through
appears also to have been the most rapidly accomplished.
Work on the Manhattan Project did not begin in earnest until
1941, though there had been a good deal of basic research
work before then, not only in the West and in Germany, but
also in the Soviet Union. By August 1945 the programme had
been carried to the point at which material for three bombs
had been produced, and two of these were used in the war
against Japan. Russian work appears to have been almost as
rapid. The first nuclear reactor built in the Soviet Union for
research purposes does not appear to have gone into operation
until the early months of 1947, but material for making an
unknown number of bombs was available by August 1949,
when the first Russian atomic weapon was exploded. It must
be inferred that Russian construction of a plutonium producing reactor (using heavy water) would also have started in
1947, and that the reactor which went into operation in the
early part of that year was intended for the testing of fuel
assemblies destined for the larger project.

Though it is unlikely that the breakneck pace of these two
development programmes will be repeated in the future, there
are some grounds for thinking that nations embarked on the
production of weapons will in many cases be anxious to

complete their development as quickly as practicable. To determine that atomic weapons are necessary for some military or political purpose and yet not to possess them must be a painful experience for any nation, and one which it must seem necessary to reduce as far as possible by pushing ahead with the production programme. But in this respect there are limits to what can be done. Even for a nation to which the recruiting of the necessary scientific and development staff would present no difficulty, it would seem to need two or three years before a production reactor could be designed with a reasonable degree of confidence. From this point construction might be expected to take at least two years, or at least three years for nations without a capacity to carry through large civil engineering projects quickly. In Britain four years went by between the coming into operation of the first testing reactor at Harwell (corresponding in design and purpose to the first Russian research reactor) and the testing of the first bomb. French development through this phase of the programme appears to have been even slower. Taking all these factors together, it would seem that an entire programme for making atomic weapons could not be completed in much less than seven years from start to finish. The accumulation of enough nuclear explosive to build large numbers of bombs will naturally take longer still.

In practice the extent to which familiarity with nuclear technology has spread round the world implies that the nations most likely to be tempted to make weapons are already part of the way along the road to achieving them. For the building and operation of research reactors and, in an increasing number of countries, power producing reactors, has provided the nucleus of skilled design and operating staff needed to mount a military programme. In some countries facilities for making nuclear materials and for processing fuel are also installed. Obviously nations with these facilities will be able to shorten the period needed to manufacture nuclear weapons. Thus countries with experience of building and operating a power reactor should be able to carry through a military programme in three or four years. In the most favourable circumstances of all, of course, nations might count on being able to divert the operation of power-producing reactors to military purposes.

This can usually be done, though a power reactor may be less efficient as a producer of military plutonium than a reactor designed explicitly for the purpose. Nevertheless fuel containing plutonium of military grade could be extracted from the reactors within a matter of months, and bombs could be made and exploded less than a year after the taking of a decision—at least if facilities for extracting the plutonium were readily available. If these had to be built specially, then there would be a delay of something like two years.

II

THE MEANS OF DELIVERY

The decision to build and test an atomic bomb must be taken in the light of a clear policy to provide a delivery system. No country has yet given serious consideration to building a bomb in a military vacuum in the hope that the prestige or terror associated with it would make the investment worthwhile. The development of the first two American bombs took place at a time when the United States had a large fleet of B-29 bombers able to carry five-ton weapons over what would now be regarded as short ranges. Since that time, American, Russian and British nuclear weapons development has been tied in closely with medium and heavy bombers and has seriously influenced their design. The Soviet Union and United States have each made a very large investment in ballistic missiles. France has confined herself to a single type of aircraft, though she has plans for a ballistic rocket which might be either land-based or submarine-based.

The possibility must nevertheless be considered that some country or countries might choose to rely on a fairly primitive delivery system or effectively none at all. A clear distinction can be made between those governments which cannot conceive any possible enemy except a highly sophisticated one (and these would include nations such as Sweden, Switzerland or Czechoslovakia) and those who might imagine warfare with more primitive powers. Japan, India or Egypt might foresee the possibility of a serious conflict with countries whose defences are neither vast nor very advanced. Such governments could probably seriously contemplate the acquisition of nuclear weapons without going to the lengths of the first four nuclear powers in assuring themselves a serious delivery system. But they would have to recognise two important limiting facts: they could not place themselves on the world stage by their acquisition of nuclear weapons; and their primitive enemies might be provided with very advanced methods of interception as a counter to their nuclear weapons programme. While the great powers are cautious about passing out offensive weapons to minor powers, they unhesitatingly provide advanced fighters and their associated radars and missiles. In short, the primitive enemy might become sophisticated for these purposes; in a world in which the great powers fear and oppose the spread, this may become virtually a certainty.

We must also consider the possibility that some governments might be attracted by the fact that nuclear weapons, of all weapons, can inflict really severe damage without any use of orthodox military methods. Left in harbours in merchant ships, hidden in embassies or moved through a country by agents, they could be weapons of terror. In all these cases, of course, there is a strong chance of being caught; and even in the most brutally amoral political climate it must be recognised that a blackmail policy of this kind would be very difficult to work. A government would have to be totally irresponsible and it is hard to see how it could practice such blackmail successfully against powers with any will to resist.

A notable characteristic of the nuclear delivery systems which have been developed up to now, unlike nuclear bombs themselves, is that they have tended to have a short life in service. It is possible that a stage might be reached with truly mobile and accurate missiles which will give them a life in the service inventory which will justify their cost. No country has yet reached this stage. At the present time, it must be assumed that the search for the really effective weapon which can be produced in great numbers at an acceptable price will go on indefinitely. A great range of projects has been undertaken in Britain and the United States and most of them have not been deployed at all or deployed in the front-line for only a short time. All were originally undertaken on the assumption that they would see at least a decade in front-line service. A small country might consider that this lavishness is due to the wealth and lack of discrimination of the countries concerned. The French have suspicions of this kind; but this line of reasoning is not justified by an examination of the facts. Such American programmes as the *Snark* or *Navaho* intercontinental unmanned bombers might well have appealed to a small nation as the correct place to put their effort. Having committed themselves heavily to them, they would probably have pushed them through to some sort of deployment; but the doubts which have led the U.S.A.F. to write off the *Navaho* and withdraw the *Snark* after a short period of service would have proved agonising to a small country which had placed itself in this position. In the end, it would undoubtedly have had to accept a level of military efficiency inferior to that which it had originally planned. The dangers of serious development problems which will delay major weapons of this kind and might radically increase the cost are always present. To insure against technical failure, new countries will have to plan their delivery systems within the limits of their existing technology. France has done this with the *Mirage 4* supersonic bomber project—something which would also be within the reach of Sweden, Canada and possibly Germany but would involve an ambitious step forward for most of the other countries which could be near the border of decision.

The experience of the nuclear powers is a guide to the possible choices of a delivery system for a new country coming into the field. The possibility that assistance might be obtained from an existing nuclear power will be discussed in the next chapter: for the moment, it will be assumed that all or most of the development and production must be done inside the country itself. Broadly, there are four alternatives:

1. A subsonic bomber, manned or unmanned
2. A supersonic bomber, manned or unmanned
3. A rocket weapon on fixed bases
4. A mobile rocket weapon

Military thought in the United States has moved through

these options from (1) to (4); Britain is trying to jump from (1) to (4) having cancelled weapons in categories (2) and (3); Russia, by contrast, seems to be concentrating on (2) and (3) though paying some attention to (4), and France has started with (2). We may expect a new nuclear power to give a great deal of thought to all of these possibilities and to assess the effort which would be required and the military effectiveness which would result. Countries which face a relatively unsophisticated adversary might, in the first instance, settle for option (1) or (2).

The new power has the advantage of the mistakes of those who have gone before. France has been able to start with a comparatively advanced delivery system. Nevertheless, the development of methods of long-range nuclear delivery can be seen clearly over the last fifteen years and the decisions which the present nuclear powers have taken about where to put their money will be studied carefully by new powers. The more they examine the possibilities, the more they are likely to realise that they have a wide technical gap to close and will probably take many years to close it.

The arrival of nuclear weapons coincided with the arrival of the jet bomber which was being given increased subsonic speed and height. In 1947–48, Britain saw the coincidence of the possibility of a medium-range four-jet bomber and her own plans for nuclear weapons and embarked on what was then the most advanced specification in the world for a jet bomber. This resulted in the Avro *Vulcan* and Handley Page *Victor* bombers (both to the same specification in case one should fail), able to fly close to the speed of sound ten miles above the earth. These types were made possible by the existence of a large and experienced aircraft industry and a world lead in jet engine technology. A less ambitious type, the *Valiant*, was developed for deployment by 1955 when a developed nuclear weapon would be ready. A supersonic bomber project, the Avro 730, was cancelled in 1957 in favour of the *Blue Streak* long-range ballistic missile. This missile was itself later cancelled.

For a new country, the requirement for a bomber would be difficult to specify and would determine the powers against which it could hope to have a deterrent effect when the nuclear force reached front-line service. Five of the present non-nuclear countries have teams in existence which have developed modern aircraft. These are Sweden, Canada, Italy, the Netherlands and Japan. Sweden is probably the best placed to build an advanced aircraft, having the Saab organisation which carried the *Draken* interceptor through to full development. Canada has allowed the team which brought the long-range supersonic Avro *Arrow* interceptor to the prototype stage to break up; but it has a substantial aircraft industry in existence. Italy has an experienced organisation in Fiat, which produced the G-91 NATO strike fighter; and both Holland and Japan have developed small turbo-prop airliners. West Germany has a potentially strong aircraft industry which is building the supersonic F–104G fighter-bomber under licence from the Lockheed Company, of California, and is developing a number of advanced projects in co-operation with American, British and French firms. All of the projects mentioned here except the *Arrow* have depended on foreign engines. No country beyond the first four nuclear powers and Canada can really be said to have made any serious effort to compete in this time-consuming and expensive technology. One of the most important bottlenecks in the whole system is undoubtedly the power-plant for a bomber or missile. Some countries such as Sweden have obtained good turbojet engines under licence for other purposes; and if these contained no restrictive clauses they would probably be able to produce engines for bombers fairly quickly. But in general it would be a long and expensive process. So far as is known, no country has made any significant progress in large rocket engines except the United States and Russia.

If it can nevertheless be assumed that good engines can be found, new countries will still have a difficult decision about what aircraft to develop to meet their minimum requirements. France and Britain, not needing great range against the predominant western areas of the Soviet Union, are each building a bomber which relies on Mach 2 flight at altitude and good low level performance to penetrate the defences of 1965–70. These are the *Mirage 4* and the British Aircraft

Corporation's TSR–2. A project of this kind seems the minimum for a new nuclear power whose enemies are sophisticated or might be equipped by a great power. It is most unlikely, however, that such a supersonic aircraft would be able to achieve intercontinental range without two in-flight refuellings; and it would probably take a country without an experienced aircraft industry a very long time.

Advocates of bomber delivery for a national nuclear weapon force may be tempted to argue that, with the great powers shifting to missiles as the main method of long-range nuclear delivery, defences against bombers are bound to decline. Thus, they might argue, the bomber will once more always get through. Either the powers will have found no defence against missiles and will have to be satisfied with the threat of retaliation as the only worthwhile defence; or they will be putting an immense effort into an anti-missile weapon at the expense of an anti-bomber defence. This argument is almost certainly fallacious. Manned bombers are (and will probably remain) the most accurate, flexible and cheap method of delivering explosives over a distant territory. They are the only sure way of destroying a target which must be sought and found, particularly if it is mobile. If by maintaining good defences the powers can be sure of destroying a high proportion of attacking bombers, they will find it in their interest to do so. There can be no serious prospect of an unopposed run for low-performance aircraft over the territory of powers of any importance. A nation contemplating the manufacture of nuclear weapons may have countries with a primitive air defence organisation among its potential enemies: and it will probably argue that any delivery system boldly and skilfully handled has some chance of escaping total destruction. Such arguments would be an unconvincing basis for a programme costing many hundreds of millions of pounds—particularly since the primitive defences of the second-class neighbour could be substantially improved and probably would be, in the face of an impending nuclear threat.

The group of countries with aircraft industries but no rocketry would obviously have to put substantially greater effort into the construction of missiles, mobile or immobile, than it would into bomber aircraft. For others, either option seems equally difficult. Even such advanced countries as Britain and France have not attempted the development undertaken by the Russians and Americans (exploiting earlier German development) between 1945 and 1961 which brought them from the V–2 with its 80 mile range and high explosive warhead to missiles carrying many megatons 9,000 miles and more. A small country following strictly in the footsteps of the Russians and Americans would have to realise that the liquid-fuelled rocket, which is far simpler to develop for heavy weapons and good accuracy, will not be effective until a high-yield warhead can be produced in a comparatively low weight. Even then, it will be immobile and so exposed to surprise attack. The difficulty of designing a warhead light enough to go into a reliable rocket and powerful enough to compensate for inaccuracy can be seen from the delays and hesitations in the early phases of the American missile programme.

If it is decided nevertheless to pursue this classic line of rocket development, a family of rocket engines is the first requirement. In the American and perhaps the Russian cases, these have grown from relatively small thrusts to larger and larger units. Test ranges for them must be built and instrumented over the required distances and an establishment for tethered running will be needed. The use of radio command guidance from the ground might free the system from the most exacting problems of inertial guidance through the use of gyroscopes, but it exposes the missile to enemy jamming and interference. Without American technical co-operation on these two points, the British *Blue Streak* programme would probably have been a 15-year undertaking costing £1,000 millions or more instead of a 10-year undertaking costing £600 millions.

Re-entry would also demand a major development effort. Much information is now published about the nose-cones which have been most successful in the United States programme, but the use of these materials would involve the development of a specialised technology. Presumably it would also be necessary to produce a high-altitude rocket for re-entry research at an early stage if the programme is an urgent one.

From the operational point of view, the lessons of American and British experience already indicate that the development of liquid-fuelled rockets is difficult to bring to a successful conclusion and that it is limited in its military value. After great expense, one obtains a large and immobile rocket which offers an excellent basis for a space programme but few advantages as a deterrent weapon. The Soviet Government may have decided that its blanket secrecy is as good a protection against crippling attack as mobility, at least as long as it can avoid aerial reconnaissance over the country. But it seems likely that no country would now embark on a programme to produce an immobile missile without great assurance about its ability to conceal the rocket bases. Even closed societies may have to deal with reconnaissance aircraft flying above their defences and only a substantial nuclear power could deter this, as the Russians have, by the threat of retaliation. It should also be noted that by the time any new nuclear power is ready to build rocket bases, both the Russians and Americans are likely to have reconnaissance satellites in orbit. A large rocket base can probably be seen even from orbital heights while it is under construction.

Thus the logic which has driven the Americans and British towards various kinds of mobile missile must be felt almost irresistibly by later nuclear powers. Of the four possibilities, this is the only one which a general staff in the early 1960s is likely to recommend as a delivery system for nuclear weapons worthy of a colossal national investment. To be mobile, a rocket must certainly use solid fuels, whose technology is more complex than that of liquid fuels and not yet fully mastered. In this as in other matters, the publication of the types of fuel which have been found to be most successful will save new countries from costly mistakes. Much has already been published by the aviation technical press and in official company releases cleared for security. The problems, nevertheless, are far more difficult than those of liquid fuels which are fully controllable through the use of pumps and electrical equipment of a familiar type. Designing a large solid mass of material to burn continuously and maintain a thrust within the needed margin is a major exercise in chemical engineering. To start

now and work a country up to something like *Minuteman*,
Pershing or *Polaris* with a warhead large enough to compensate
for inaccuracy might take a country twenty years or more on
its own. It would not be surprising to find that one or two
countries were quietly working in this field on a small peaceful
rocket programme so as to have some technology on which to
build at a later date. But to start on a front-line weapon at this
stage would mean giving many years of notice to anyone who
might be concerned.

One estimate which the present nuclear powers had to make
at quite an early stage of their design for a delivery system was
the rate of nuclear weapons development they would achieve.
One characteristic of British and American development is
that early rockets were made larger than was needed. This
was particularly true of *Blue Streak*, which obtained considerable free warhead capacity after the opening of the American
atomic secrets to Britain in 1958. But at the design stage
governments have always chosen a large rocket rather than
risk the possibility of ending an expensive programme with no
weapon at all. The way to avoid this is to wait until the
weapons programme is very far advanced before deciding on
the final specification for a vehicle to carry the bomb. This
suggests an even longer period of gestation. Twenty years is
probably modest. The United States, after all, will have taken
from 1942 to 1962 to develop the Manhattan Project into the
Minuteman. Britain would have taken from 1946 to 1965 to
produce the immobile *Blue Streak* in spite of its American
rocket engine and guidance system. For a delivery system of
any size, the British figure of £500 millions for the V-bomber
force and £600 millions (planned) for underground deployment of *Blue Streak* at least gives some idea of what may have to
be spent by a country even with a broadly based weapons
industry already in existence.

Chapter 2

International Co-operation

TO attain nuclear power independently is difficult. This is the thread running through the last chapter, in which it was suggested that even in countries as technically advanced, and as prosperous, as Britain and France, the task of becoming and of remaining a serious nuclear power is likely to be a strain. For smaller countries the physical obstacles loom even larger. It is no wonder that in their assessment of the feasibility of the goal, nations will consider what help might be obtained from others. The possibility that bombs might be purchased outright will be investigated as will the prospects of ready-made delivery systems. There can be no doubt that the process of becoming a nuclear power could be hastened and made easier at every stage by appropriate and timely assistance from abroad. So cogent are these considerations, indeed, that there are grounds for believing that the future spread of nuclear weapons throughout the world will be influenced considerably by the extent to which the established nuclear powers are willing to assist other countries.

The subject of this chapter is the kind of technical assistance with the manufacture of nuclear weapons which is available at the present time. The manufacture of nuclear explosives is considered first, and an attempt is made to estimate how much assistance in nuclear technology a would-be nuclear power might obtain. Means by which nations might obtain nuclear delivery systems for their own use are considered separately and attention is then given to the various international agreements for siting nuclear weapons on allied territory.

I

TECHNICAL ASSISTANCE WITH NUCLEAR EXPLOSIVES

The United States has set its face against helping other nations with the manufacture of nuclear explosives. Russian policy is harder to discern, but seems similar in objectives. The difference was exemplified immediately after World War II when the United States proposed to the United Nations that the spread of nuclear weapons to other countries should be limited by the Baruch Plan, and when the Soviet Union declared that this was nothing but a scheme to preserve for the West a perpetual monopoly in nuclear weapons. American policy on nuclear collaboration with other nations has been characterised by an attempt rigorously to account for every gram of fissile material that might change hands. The Soviet Union, by contrast, has consistently argued that such attempts interfere intolerably with national sovereignty. Nevertheless Russian policy appears to have been directed to the same goal, and to have had the same effect.

However, both nations have in the last eight years done a great deal to add to the now substantial body of publicly available information about nuclear technology. The formal impetus for this development was President Eisenhower's 'Atoms for Peace Campaign' launched at the United Nations in December, 1953. Both in the basic science of the subject and in fields such as the design of nuclear reactors, much information of value to potential designers of military production reactors is now freely available in published literature. It should, however, be recognised that this would not free these designers from the need to create for themselves the development programmes without which a nuclear reactor could not be brought safely into commission, and that there are good reasons for thinking that this step is likely to be a more difficult one than would be the theoretical design study for a military reactor. The willingness of the two great powers to part with previously secret information about nuclear technology in the mid-fifties was probably fortified as much by a cold recognition that secrets would not keep for ever as by the wish—then also an important influence on policy—to share with smaller nations the potential benefits of peaceful nuclear power.

The policy of the United States towards the provision of assistance to other countries in nuclear technology was first codified by the Atomic Energy Act of 1946, more commonly known as the MacMahon Act. This was an extremely restrictive document, aimed at preventing the dissemination of information about nuclear technology, in order to prevent the spread of nuclear weapons. The terms of the original Act on 'Control of Information' convey the spirit of the legislation:

'It shall be the policy of the Atomic Energy Commission to control the dissemination of restricted data in such a manner as to ensure the common defence and security. Consistent with such policy, the Commission shall be guided by the following principles: That until Congress declares by joint resolution that effective and enforceable international safeguards against the use of atomic energy for destructive purposes have been established, there shall be no exchange of information with other nations with respect to the use of atomic energy for industrial purposes . . .'[1]

Not until 1951 was this restrictive provision qualified by granting the Commission the right 'when in its unanimous judgement the common defence and security would be substantially promoted' to make agreements to exchange data on reactor metallurgy and construction. The communication of restricted data on the design and fabrication of atomic weapons was explicitly forbidden. As is noted in the next chapter those provisions of the MacMahon Act which were intended explicitly to prevent the spread of nuclear weapons did in fact reinforce British determination to become a separate nuclear power. This paradoxical consequence is often characteristic of restrictive legislation.

The first important relaxation of the Act came in 1954, when it was substantially recast. This was the beginning of the "Atoms for Peace" era, and the new legislation was meant to enable exchanges of information between the United States and other countries on the peaceful uses of atomic energy. The sale of nuclear equipment for use in such things as power reactors was also foreseen, as was the supply of fuel for them. For the first time the atomic energy legislation permitted the United States Department of Defense to communicate to other nations information on such things as training for atomic warfare. Information about the design of weapons could not be

[1] Section 10(a).

passed on to other nations, though 'external characteristics including size, weight, shape, yields and effects, and systems used in the delivery and use thereof' became communicable for the first time. The 1954 revision of the Act saw the beginning of a period during which some dozens of bilateral agreements on co-operation in peaceful fields were signed between the United States and other nations.

Although an Anglo-American defence bilateral agreement was signed in 1955, the first use of the provisions of the new Act relating to military uses of atomic energy came with an agreement with the United Kingdom on July 3rd, 1958. Similar agreements have now been signed with Australia, Canada, France, West Germany, Greece, the Netherlands, Turkey and Italy. Though all of these agreements except those with Australia, France and Greece are in part secret, there is good reason to believe that none of them goes further than to permit sensible co-ordination on military planning between military allies. The agreement with Italy was, for example, a necessary prelude to the siting of IRBMs in that country.

The only exception so far to the rule that the United States will not provide information or materials for use in atomic weapons or in their design is embodied in the agreement with the United Kingdom which was further expanded on July 18th, 1959. This permitted the disclosure of details about the design of nuclear weapons in the United States, and for the exchange of fissile material between the United States and the United Kingdom—but in such a fashion that the numerical strength of the British stockpile cannot by this means be increased above the level which it could reach with the use of existing British facilities for making fissile material. In practice it is most probable that this provision of the agreement between the two countries was intended to permit the exchange of British plutonium for American fissile uranium. So far as the design of bombs is concerned, it would appear that the flow of information between the two countries is free. Britain formally qualified for exemption from the restrictive provisions of the Act by reasons of having both a nuclear weapon stockpile, and an effective strategic delivery capability.

The special agreement on nuclear sharing with Britain was

made possible by a comprehensive amendment to the 1954 Atomic Energy Act, which became law on July, 1958. Though this amendment does not permit the actual supply of completed nuclear weapons by the United States, it does enable the AEC to make agreements with allied governments for the supply of information about the design of nuclear weapons and of material such as fissile uranium. However, the amendment required that these exchanges should only take place in circumstances where they were necessary to improve 'atomic weapon design, development and fabrication capacity' in the country receiving them, and also if that country 'has made substantial progress in the development of atomic weapons'. An agreement along these lines was introduced as soon as the amendment became law. In 1958, it was assumed that the agreement with the United Kingdom might in due course be followd by similar agreements with other countries. No American ally has since demonstrated 'substantial progress in the development of atomic weapons', and it now seems as if the agreement with Britain will remain an isolated exception to American policy.

The severity of the restrictions placed on the use of American material supplied for peaceful purposes to countries other than Britain is exemplified by the agreement with the Euratom organisation which preceded the largely abortive mutual agreement for the development of certain types of nuclear reactors in Europe. The signature of the agreement was accompanied by a 'memorandum of understanding' which says that 'both Euratom and the United States recognise the extreme importance of assuring that all activities under the joint programme shall be directed solely toward the peaceful uses of atomic energy'. The document goes on to record a 'guarantee by Euratom that no material supplied by the United States as a part of the programme'—either fissile material or equipment such as reactor components—shall be used 'for atomic weapons, or for research on or development of atomic weapons, or for any other military purpose'. The same undertaking specifies that material—such as 'plutonium —which might be produced by or in the use of 'materials and equipment supplied under the agreement' shall also not be used for military purposes. To ensure that these conditions are satisfied, the agreement also lays it down that the Euratom organisation shall establish a system of inspection and control (which has now been done) equipped to examine the designs of all equipment using material supplied under the programme of co-operation. It is empowered to demand operating records from all plants using material of American origin or fissile material (such as plutonium) manufactured with the help of American material; it is obliged to store any fissile material not actually being used as part of a peaceful atomic power programme, and which has been manufactured with the help of American material, in some special facility; and its teams of inspectors have the right of access to all places, data and 'to any person who by reason of his occupation deals with equipment, devices or facilities safeguarded under this agreement'.

There is every reason to think that stipulations like these will actually prevent the diversion of material supplied for peaceful purposes into military channels. At the same time there is no evidence that United States insistence on such rigid safeguards has seriously hampered the development of peaceful atomic energy in other countries. To be sure there have been times when Britain and France could have profited in their civilian developments from the supply of materials such as enriched uranium, but this deprivation has probably had no lasting effect.

American policies aimed at the control of information rather than of materials have been less successful, though through no fault of those who drafted the legislation on the subject. Rather it is that attempts to limit the diffusion of technological information are almost certain, in the long run, to be frustrated. However well-designed a security system may be, leakage of information either by deliberate espionage or by accident must be expected to erode the integrity of secrets. Then it is possible for people without access to secret information to discover a great deal about the manufacture of nuclear weapons. The way in which the character of the thermonuclear weapon exploded at Bikini in the Pacific (March 1954) was inferred by the calculations of private citizens in the United

States, the United Kingdom and in Japan is evidence of the difficulty of keeping at least the most spectacular secrets. But it is also the case that, with the steady (and rapid) increase of technological sophistication, feats which could only be accomplished with difficulty during the hectic years of the Manhattan Project may come to seem comparatively easy, even to powers other than those now possessed of atomic weapons. In this spirit it is, for example, reasonable to predict that the still closely (and successfully) guarded secrets about the technology of gaseous diffusion plants for making enriched uranium are likely to find wide currency within a decade or so. Yet these tendencies cannot be prevented by the design of legislation. The learning (and relearning) of this truth has been a painful process and not merely in the United States.

The policy of the Soviet Union on the sharing of military nuclear technology is much less explicit than that of the United States. Its objects are also somewhat obscure; and at least some confusion on this account springs from repeated Russian insistence that to impose controls on the uses made of nuclear materials within a nation's territory is a kind of 'colonialist' interference with its sovereignty. This charge appears to have been born out of Russian anxiety to break the United States monopoly in atomic weapons after the Second World War. The Russian argument leans heavily on the unsubstantiated assertion that restrictions on the free use of nuclear material must necessarily limit the peaceful use which can be made of of them, or indeed of atomic power in general. In fact, with three exceptions, the atomic reactors built in satellite countries (and in Egypt and Yugoslavia) with assistance from the Soviet Union are intended primarily for research. Both China and Yugoslavia received by 1958 research reactors working at a power level of 6,500 kW., and comparable in many ways to the reactors built for the testing of construction materials at Harwell in England and at other nuclear research centres in Europe. Somewhat earlier, satellite countries in Eastern Europe were each provided with a research reactor working at 2000 kW. It has been agreed that Czechoslovakia, East Germany and Hungary should be provided with reactors for the production of electricity (in amounts of 150,000 kW,

70,000 kW. and 100,000 kW. respectively). It is no accident that the three countries concerned are among the most prolific sources of uranium ore within the Eastern bloc, for though a Soviet lien on this material is ensured by trading agreements, there has at various times been friction between the satellites and the Soviet Union apparently arising out of a sense of un-just exploitation of a valuable national asset.

The amounts of enriched uranium provided as fuel for the research reactors are too small to be significant from a military point of view. Even though formal agreements about what shall happen to spent fuel have not been published, there is evidence that recipient nations return their spent fuel to its original supplier. This is no doubt encouraged by the recognition that further supplies might only be provided as spent fuel was returned.

On the exchange of information, the Soviet Union is somewhat more forthcoming than in the supply of fuel for reactors. The nuclear research institute at Dubna near Moscow is in reality a co-operative research station and the costs are paid for by subscription from among the satellite nations. Of the total budget some 40 per cent is provided by the Soviet itself, China pays 20 per cent, and East Germany and Poland each pay nearly seven per cent. Much of the work of the institute is concerned with fundamental physics and would be relevant to the production of atomic weapons only to the extent that it provides training. It is also provided with research reactors, but these could never be used as a complete substitute for those normally required by a programme of military production.

One aspect of the relationship between the Soviet Union and her allies in the supply of nuclear materials may have an important bearing on the future of the spread of nuclear weapons. Russian control over dependent countries by controlling their supplies of nuclear raw materials at source must become more difficult if substantial programmes for the peaceful exploitation of nuclear power are mounted in the satellite countries. Much larger quantities of fuel would then be involved. The possibilities of reprocessing spent fuel outside the Soviet Union would become economically attractive, and in these circumstances it would be surprising if the Soviet Union did not have to adopt more formal agreements (similar to the American bilateral agreements) for controlling supplies of nuclear fuel and other materials. The same result may be brought about by a demand for access to domestic ore supplies such as was made during the Hungarian uprising of 1956. On that occasion the right to their own Hungarian uranium ore featured prominently among the demands of the insurgents, and the Soviet Union afterwards recognised—formally at least—that there would have to be a more liberal system for exploiting Hungarian ores.

British policy on the sharing of nuclear equipment and information closely resembles the American. Bilateral agreements are signed with the recipients of nuclear fuel and equipment (Japan and Italy are the two nations so far supplied with substantial quantities). The right is reserved to carry out inspections at the sites at which this equipment and material is used. It should be recognised that the facilities exist in the host country and are kept from military uses only by the sanctions of international law.

The other important source of direct assistance in the manufacture of atomic weapons at present is France. Nothing has been said about the agreement with Israel under which a French nuclear reactor is being constructed in the Negev; but there is every sign that the French authorities do not share the view of the American and British Governments that aid to allies in producing bombs is a bad thing. Having struggled to establish their own right to nuclear weapons in defiance of a ring which was steadily closing, they are still influenced by arguments that the more weapons spread the more stable the world will become. The French do not quite respond to the anti-colonialist slogans favoured in these matters by the Indians and Russians; but there is something of this attitude in their effort to defy what they regard as a restrictive and exclusive Anglo-Saxon club over the whole range of diplomacy. They seem to see the limitation of nuclear sharing to peaceful purposes as one aspect of this.

Elsewhere restrictive arrangements had been made by the Governments of both West Germany and the Netherlands on the free exchange of information about the process for enriching uranium in its fissile content by the use of gas centrifuges. The need for such a restriction was urged on the two Governments by those of the United States and the United Kingdom, after it had become plain that technical developments had conspired to brighten the prospects of the centrifuge process as a means of enriching uranium.

Restrictions on the use which may be made of nuclear materials are by now conspicuous features of international agreements for collaboration in atomic energy, at least in the West. The setting up of a scheme for the physical control of plant and material was, for example, required in the Rome Treaty which established the Euratom organisation. The creation of this control system was also one of the conditions laid down by the United States as a pre-requisite of collaboration in the development of certain types of industrial reactors. But though the objective of the Rome Treaty, and of the control organisation which has now been established, is to prevent the military use of materials or assistance made available to individual nations through the international organisation, there is nothing in this machinery which prevents a nation from becoming a nuclear power. The fact that France has not found its membership of Euratom inconsistent with its manufacture of atomic weapons is a practical demonstration of this.

Even so it should not be thought that French resolution to manufacture nuclear weapons has fitted in easily with the establishment of the Euratom control system. Thus, for example, one of the original requirements of the system of controls was that nations should submit to the control agency details of the capacity of each of their production plants (such as reactors) and also information about the use made of these, (which bears directly on the amounts of plutonium which these have actually produced). In practice it has turned out that the French Government has considered itself able to provide the Euratom Commission with details of the capacity of its factories for making military plutonium, but unable to supply details of how these have been operated and so to provide a guide (however confidential) to the actual plutonium production. If—as seems likely—the United Kingdom will soon belong to the Euratom organisation, a similar laxity in the control regulations will be necessary to accommodate British military production of nuclear explosives.

The International Atomic Energy Agency (IAEA) at Vienna is more directly relevant to discussions of the spread of nuclear weapons. Indeed the creation of some means for controlling the uses to which nuclear materials are put is required by the statute which established the International Agency in 1956. As things stand however it has no control over the dissemination of expertise in nuclear technology.

The provision of the IAEA's statute which requires that a control organ shall be established were implemented only after two years of negotiations by the executive body of the agency (the Board of Governors). These led in the spring of 1960 to a provisional system of control and inspection of materials and equipment provided as technical assistance through the Agency. Since the United States delegates to the Agency played the principal part in designing these safeguards, it is not surprising that they should resemble closely in many respects the kinds of safeguards required in the bilateral treaties on nuclear cooperation signed with several other nations.

In practice, however, the adoption of the regulations so far promulgated by the International Agency is only provisional. The intention is that these shall be reviewed after they have been tried out for a period of two years (in March 1963). It is also recognised that the safeguards against the use of nuclear materials for military purposes shall apply only to nuclear reactors which are not capable of producing more than 100,000 kW. of power in the form of heat—just a half of the output of heat from one of the French plutonium producing reactors (G2 and G3). Though modifications of this proviso may be practicable when experience has accumulated, the fact remains that the Agency's system for control and safeguarding is at present somewhat limited.

The principles of the safeguards system designed at Vienna are that this shall apply not merely to materials such as uranium, but also the equipment such as reactors where, 'in the opinion of the Board', these are 'substantially assisted' by the Agency. So far as fuel is concerned, safeguards only apply to material supplied by the Agency, but a nation shall have the right to be exempt from control if its total stocks of nuclear materials are smaller than prescribed quantities (e.g. 10 metric tons for natural uranium and 200 grams for plutonium or for fully enriched uranium). In general reactors are exempt from control if they produce fewer than 3000 kW. of power, though the Agency has the right to impose controls on items of equipment which could be used to further military ends (among which, no doubt, must be included assemblies of enriched uranium not large enough to explode but sufficient to provide information of value in the design of nuclear weapons). Except when these provisions exempt materials or equipment from control, the International Agency has the right to require advance information on the design and uses to which equipment or material is to be put and regular reports about the use actually made of it; and it has the right to carry out regular inspections of the facilities concerned. Agency control would apply to nuclear fuel whenever this is obtained with its assistance, or even when material with some other origin is used in a facility to which Agency safeguards attach. Safeguards would, however, be applied to installations such as reactors only when these contained fuel subject to the safeguards procedure. The number of inspections of reactors to be carried out in a year is specified in terms of the capacity of these plants to produce plutonium. As a rough guide, the regulations specify that there should be one inspection whenever a reactor could have produced the equivalent of some five kilograms of plutonium.

One feature of the provisional regulations is that nuclear fuel returned to some other state for reprocessing, or to some uncontrolled facility within the same state, shall be exempted from control so long as an equivalent amount of fissile material is placed under control. The intention of this provision is to enable nations such as the United States to reprocess material from abroad in plants used for military purposes. It also makes it possible for nations to make use of their own military installations to reprocess material supplied through the international agency for peaceful purposes. Although this provision merely takes account of the fact that nations such as the United States are unlikely to undertake the worthwhile task of reprocessing fuel from countries abroad if, by so doing, they are required to open up their secret military establishments, the effect has been to strengthen criticism of the discriminatory character of the system of safeguards adopted at Vienna. Within the Agency and elsewhere, the Soviet Union has been at pains to emphasise the way in which the Vienna safeguards threaten to infringe the sovereignty of states receiving assistance from the Agency. Mme Z. V. Mironova said in the United Nations at the end of 1961 that 'such controls serve certain circles who wish to keep all resources of uranium in their own hands, to control its production and fix prices that would be advantageous to United States monopolies. It is quite obvious that no self-respecting state would wish to sell its sovereignty for a few kilograms of plutonium'.[1]

The Soviet objections to the Vienna safeguards system were fully argued by Mr. Molotov—the delegate to Vienna—in the debate on the matter in the Administrative and Legal Committee of the Agency in November 1960. He said that one of the objects of the agency had been to ensure that all countries would have access to nuclear materials even if these could not be obtained on a bilateral basis, but the effect of the safeguards system was to permit countries with access to these materials to retain a right of discrimination against others seeking assistance. He went on to argue that the safeguards were not a means 'of preventing the appearance of new countries possessing nuclear weapons' because they did not prevent the manufacture of atomic weapons, and to claim that the proposals for control on nuclear equipment were cast too widely if security of control against the diversion of nuclear material to military purposes was the only objective of policy. In the same debate Mr. Molotov urged that the frequency of inspections for the diversion of nuclear material to military ends should be linked to the industrial capacity of the nation concerned, and also argued that the proposals for carrying out the inspection procedures had not been properly worked out. Though Russian opposition to the system of controls now appears to be implacable, this has not always been true. At the beginning of the discussions at Vienna on the system of controls

[1] *New York Times*, November 24th, 1961.

it appeared that the Russian delegates were prepared to work towards a still more stringent system than that which has now been adopted, and it was not until the beginning of 1959, when it became apparent how great a degree of detailed control over production plants would be needed, that Russian opposition to the Vienna scheme began to crystallise.

Before that time opposition to the system of controls had been voiced at Vienna and elsewhere by the representatives of India, who argued that controls of the kind proposed were unacceptable so long as they did not also apply to the great powers. In 1959 the Russians took this thesis as the main theme of their attitude towards the Vienna proposals. It is doubtful whether either the Russian or the Indian view should be considered as entirely honest. Thus there is no reason to think that the Russians would—in their present mood—consent to detailed inspection of their own nuclear production plants.

This conflict embodies the irony of international science in a nationalist world—in particular the difficulty which arises because free trade and exchange of nuclear materials is incompatible with the legitimate wish of some nations to ensure that technical assistance they provide to other nations, whether directly or through the International Agency, shall not be used for military purposes. It may be illusory to claim, as some in the West have done, that the Vienna system of safeguards will ensure that the possession of nuclear weapons does not spread. But the safeguards do at least imply that technical assistance through the international agency cannot hasten the process by which nations may independently acquire nuclear power. Within this assurance, however, it would be as well if some of the internal defects of the system of safeguards proposed at Vienna (and pointed out by the Russians) could be more openly recognised in the West. Matters like the rights and responsibilities of the international inspectors are, for example, only poorly worked out.

The present situation at Vienna is that the safeguards system has been adopted for a provisional period, and that it is being applied to a number of small transactions in nuclear fuel within the agency. Thus, for example, three tons of fuel supplied to Japan by Canada through the Agency are now (though not originally) under the safeguards procedure. So are quantities of fuel for research reactors in Finland and in Norway. In addition the United States has agreed to place four of its domestic reactors under the Agency control and safeguards procedure, as a means of testing the safeguards procedures. So far as the future of the safeguards system is concerned, it is conceivable that no vestige of the present system will survive the current trial period. If it does, substantial modifications of the present arrangement may be needed, and chief among these is probably the need to extend the safeguards to power reactors of the kinds likely to be useful in the production of military explosives. So great are the divisions between the East and West over several issues of agency policy, among which the safeguards system is only one, that the survival of the Agency itself is often considered to be in doubt.

II

TECHNICAL ASSISTANCE WITH DELIVERY SYSTEMS

While this effort has gone into safeguarding fissile materials, very little effort has gone into limiting the spread of systems or components which are essential to the construction of delivery systems. Aero-engines sell freely on the world markets from British, French or American factories. Russian engines are available to Communist countries and probably to others. Such effective nuclear weapon carriers as the British *Canberra* bomber or the American F-104G fighter-bomber have been sold as complete systems to a wide variety of countries. Communist countries and such neutral countries as Egypt and Indonesia have been able to obtain advanced bombers such as the Il-28 or the *Badger* from the Soviet Union. It must be said, however, that all the cases of the sale of bombers have been by a leading nuclear power to a non-nuclear power which showed no sign of wanting the bombers to carry nuclear weapons. Nations seeking a carrier for a nuclear bomb might find the bargaining more difficult.

Although several types of bomber have been sold or built under licence for conventional purposes, this does not apply to any of the modern front line bombers of the United States, Russia and Britain. The British *Canberra* jet bomber has been sold to the New Zealand, Rhodesian, Indian and Peruvian air forces and has been built under licence in Australia (as well as the United States). Details of its bomb load have never been released, but those used by the Royal Air Force are known to carry the smaller British atomic bombs. It has been said that the Mark 8 *Canberra* carries six 1,000 pound conventional bombs, so it is a fair assumption that it could carry up to 8,000 pounds in weapons weight. The twin-jet Ilyushin Il–28 (known in the West as the *Beagle*) has had a similar history in Russian service, though the bomb load is thought to be something under 5,000 pounds. These are to be found in the air forces of Poland, Rumania, Hungary, China, the United Arab Republic and Indonesia. These light bombers are now considerably slower than the interceptors in service in even quite small air forces, but their bomb load would make them a possible carrier for nuclear weapons. The only case so far of the sale of medium bombers concerns the Russian Tu–16 *Badger*, which has been made available to Indonesia and to Egypt. As far as the policy of the British and American governments are concerned, there is no knowing whether they would sell such aircraft to an aspiring nuclear power.

For the time scale which India or Canada or Sweden would now be contemplating (an operational bomb by say 1970 and after), it is most unlikely that a major investment in a subsonic delivery system would be acceptable. If a bomber was considered desirable, most military staffs would ask for an aircraft with at least limited supersonic performance. In the West, this would confine them to the American B–58 *Hustler*, the British TSR–2, or the French *Mirage* 4. The Russians have a wider choice (to judge from the 1961 Tushino air display) with at least three supersonic bombers. The Chinese Air Force might be interested in these aeroplanes and so might the Indian Air Force.

While examining this question, the free access of virtually the whole world to long range airliners should not be over-

looked. Most countries of consequence already own a number
of Boeing 707, Douglas DC–8 or other airliners capable of
flying at 550 m.p.h. over ranges up to about 4,000 miles. Other
important subsonic jets such as the British *Comet 4* or the
French *Caravelle* have good medium range performance and
the Russian Tu–104, which is a direct development of the
Badger bomber, and the Tu–114, a development of the *Bear*
bomber, should not be overlooked. A French or Anglo-French
supersonic airliner may well be in service by 1970. The largest
of these airliners will carry payloads of 15–30 tons and so
should be quite adequate to accommodate two atomic bombs.
They do not, of course, have a bomb bay; but recent announce-
ments that spare engines can be carried inboard under the
wings make it clear that the stressing is good enough on the
Boeing 707 and DC–8, at least, to take a weight of 5,000
pounds under each wing while maintaining civil aviation
safety margins.

The present trend towards self-contained navigational systems in civil airliners makes them more valuable as bombers.
Doppler navigation techniques originally refined for R.A.F.
Bomber Command are, for example, now being applied in a
wide variety of civil types. Ground mapping radar which is
becoming standard would help in making a final run on to a
target. It may be doubted whether anything more would be
needed to permit an air force to make a fairly accurate attack
with a nuclear weapon on to an enemy target. The main
elements of a subsonic long-range military bombing force are
now available on the civil market and should be watched carefully if any country appears to be considering a programme
for what is in effect a blackmail bomb.

While the Boeing 707 might be inferior in performance as a
military weapon to the B–58 which was produced at much the
same time, it is undoubtedly superior to the aircraft which a
smaller nuclear power might try to produce to a similar time
scale. Above all, there are no uncertainties about its success.
Its promise is a sure and tested fact and its engines and systems
have vast development resources behind them. The possibility
is therefore not quite so fanciful as it may sound. Among the
countries of particular interest to this study, the following

numbers of Boeing 707s, DC–8s, de Havilland *Comet* 4s, Sud *Caravelles* and *Britannias* are in service: Canada 23, Sweden 21, Italy 16, Australia 10, Argentina 8, Switzerland 7, Brazil 6, Japan 5, India 4, and Israel 4.

The only cases of direct sale of delivery systems to nuclear powers are found inside the special conditions of the Anglo-American alliance. Following the cancellation of the *Blue Streak* long-range rocket in 1960, the British Government sought and obtained general agreement to the provision of advanced American solid-fuel rockets for the modernisation of its heavy nuclear force. President Eisenhower agreed in principle with Mr. Macmillan, the Prime Minister, that they would make the air-launched *Skybolt* missile available in 1965 and the submarine-launched *Polaris* available in 1970. Britain has taken an active option on the first of these while reserving judgement on the second. Adaptation of the Mark 2 version of the *Vulcan* bomber to take *Skybolt* is going ahead; and the Douglas Company, which is building the missile at Culver City, California, is putting considerable design effort at British expense into ensuring its compatibility with the *Vulcan* as well as the American B–52G and H bombers for which it was originally designed. The United States has not agreed to supply nuclear warheads to Britain: that remains excluded by the Atomic Energy Act. But since it is free to provide designs, information and materials, it is obviously making it possible for the Atomic Energy Authority in Britain to build the same warheads as the basic American design for *Skybolt*. Britain would undoubtedly have to sacrifice either range or yield if she had to rely on her own designs and the effectiveness of the whole system might be reduced to the point where it could not be made airborne. With the exception of the *Skybolt* and *Polaris* understandings with Britain, it seems clear that easy conditions of sale do not prevail for modern missiles—and there are signs that the United States may be unwilling to sell *Polaris* if Britain decides to adopt it.

Looking more broadly at the Anglo-American case, it should be noted that technical co-operation of the most advanced kind took place long before the amendments to the Atomic Energy Act of 1958, which virtually dismantled the wall of secrecy between America and Britain. In 1954–55, the United States Government allowed the Rocketdyne Division of North American Aviation to enter into a licence agreement with Rolls-Royce Limited, of England, under which all the engineering details of the only large rocket engine then at an advanced stage of development in the United States were made freely available. From this S–3 engine, which was basically the rocket which was to boost the cancelled *Navaho* and had been adapted to the *Atlas* ballistic missiles, Rolls-Royce built up the *Blue Streak* powerplant. As a direct parallel to this, an advanced and expensive American system of inertial guidance using gyroscopes was put into production under licence in Britain and a great deal was learned about the engineering of large rockets and heat problems of re-entry. These arrangements are particularly significant because there was no ambiguity about the purposes of the weapon. The cancellation of *Blue Streak* as a military weapon in 1960 does not affect the importance of these arrangements as a sign of what has been done at least once between close allies.

One other Anglo-American arrangement should also be examined. This is the series of co-operative agreements about nuclear reactors for submarines. Nuclear submarines take a peculiarly ambiguous place in the problem of the spread of nuclear weapons because they are driven by atomic energy without being nuclear weapons while providing the most complex part of the platform of a particularly advanced nuclear delivery system. A spread of atomic propulsion information is comparable to the sharing of advanced jet engines: it allows new countries to make more advanced vehicles for conventional warfare or for nuclear warfare. Nevertheless, the Atomic Energy Act prohibited such sharing and the remarkable world lead obtained by the United States with the *Nautilus* reactor made her allies very anxious to avoid duplication. American policy planners have obviously been in a dilemma on this question. In 1957, before the major amendment to the Atomic Energy Act, an agreement for sharing with Britain in marine nuclear power was signed and ratified without objections in Congress. At that time, Britain was well-advanced on her own marine nuclear power plant which was then substantially re-designed to incorporate American experience. Things were taken a step farther when the U.S. Government agreed to allow the sale of a completed American reactor for the first British nuclear submarine, the *Dreadnought*. Britain adhered to her previous plans to produce a British nuclear engine for her second and successive nuclear submarines. In spite of the possibility of a batch of missile-firing submarines in the Royal Navy after 1970, the immediate requirement for nuclear power by the British was for submarines carrying torpedoes and doing the conventional maritime job required by the NATO Atlantic command. The spread of these engines is not, therefore, a spread of nuclear weapons; but as with the 'atoms for peace' programme it spreads technology and as with aero-engines it provides an important part of a certain kind of nuclear weapons system.

The French experience with the Americans has been markedly different from the British. Like Britain, France requested and was refused information about nuclear weapons while her own programme was in the preliminary stages, but at least twice she has been refused the same treatment as was given to Britain at the same stage of development. Although General de Gaulle has made it clear that he is as ready to buy his *force de frappe* as to build it, neither the United States nor the United Kingdom has made any offers to sell weapons, aeroplanes or rockets to their NATO ally. Washington has been particularly unforthcoming. According to the *New York Times*[1], Mr. Dulles, the Secretary of State, promised an atomic powerplant to the French Government for their proposed submarine in 1959, but then had to withdraw the offer when the Joint Congressional Committee on Atomic Energy objected that this very important American technical lead might leak through France to the Soviet Union. The reasons given at the time did not raise the question of the spread of weapons; but they marked out for the first time in the post-war era a clear distinction in the atomic relations of the United States and Britain on the one hand and the United States and another major ally on the other.

The other important contrast between the American policy

[1] March 15th, 1959.

towards Britain and that towards France concerns rockets. Where the United States made an advanced rocket of the day available to the British in 1955 (as described), she did not do the same thing for France. Despite French ingenuity with small rockets, the French IRBM intended for 1970 has been said to depend on the prospect of American co-operation. As with the marine nuclear powerplant, this co-operation looked hopeful enough in the early days and then inexplicably disappeared. Licence agreements of the greatest promise were cancelled and the French must now face the prospect of constructing the second generation of the *force de frappe*, like the first, from their own resources or (possibly in a European context) with British assistance.

The contrast in the British and French cases suggests the true political foundation of American policy on nuclear sharing. Because of the needs of alliance and the habit of legalism, the Atomic Energy Act makes substantial progress in nuclear weapons, a technical issue, the key to sharing. In truth, the issue is overwhelmingly political: the United States will not at present share its atomic secrets with any country which it can imagine using them in circumstances of which it would not approve. However the issue may be blurred by diplomacy, the Americans trust the British far more than they trust the French. This was probably increased rather than decreased by Suez, the one major break in Anglo-American relations since 1941. For it was then the British accepted, in humiliation, the fact that in the face of American opposition they could not go on. France did nothing of the kind; nor have the French over the years been prepared to give the Americans the same free hand on their territory as Britain has done. This became public when in 1960 American fighter-bombers had to be moved to Britain and Germany to permit their re-equipment with nuclear weapons; but on day to day matters it has been obvious to both governments for years.

In general it is possible to draw the following conclusions about American policy:

(1) Full exchanges such as exist with the United Kingdom are only likely to come about where there is a fundamental

and long-term sense of unity (combined with an advanced domestic weapons industry) apparent both to the Administration and to Congress. This might develop in time with other members of American-led alliances—continental Europe, Japan or Australia, for example—but only after many years of unchanging policy and political stability had convinced the Administration and the Joint Congressional Committee that the alliance in question had become immutable.

(2) Non-nuclear components for aircraft delivery systems are probably available to allies, though a complete bomber aircraft might be difficult to get.

(3) Non-nuclear components for missiles as delivery systems are probably not available to allies who have not achieved the intimacy described in (1), though there is little experience on which to judge.

Politically, this policy will be difficult to sustain with allies if the alliance comes to depend heavily on American requests for aid and support rather than the reverse. In a world in which conventional military power is becoming more important, the United States may become more of a petitioner than a supplier. If areas of the world in which America's allies have comparatively minor interests (such as South America) become central concerns, the successive American Administrations might find themselves tempted to bargain for military and economic support in these areas with the offer of more intimate sharing. There have so far been no signs of this.

There is one more important category of sharing which should not be overlooked. This might be called operational sharing and can create a permanent dependence of the small atomic power on the large one in a way that other forms of sharing do not. Perhaps the most important aspect of operational sharing is intelligence in the broadest sense. A nuclear power will be anxious to have day-to-day contact with the most advanced thinking and with the probable threat which faces it from its enemies. The middle powers are ill-equipped to provide themselves with a substantial flow of information about the disposition of the forces of those they fear, the progress of their technology, and the most effective way of using their delivery systems. Obviously, the close co-operation between Royal Air Force Bomber Command and the United States Strategic Air Command is of considerable value to the former. This has now progressed from the exchange of broad categories of information to the sharing of tactical warning which the British have not chosen to develop themselves. Where the radar system on which British fighters and anti-aircraft guided weapons depend is national, the Ballistic Missile Early Warning System is American with a small British participation. The two countries are sharing all the information with BMEWS (with its first three stations in Alaska, Greenland and England, covering the northern approaches to Britain and North America). Britain has also offered the use of her soil for a ground station for the American *Midas* satellite system and will receive the tactical warning which it is hoped these orbiting heat-sensors will offer. Britain could probably have constructed her own BMEWS system, though she would not have expected the same warning time if it was not linked into a more extensive chain. It may be doubted whether the expense of *Midas* would be within her reasonable means.

This opens up a general problem for middle powers. It is easy enough to know what time has shown is needed in front-line service now; but only countries which took gambles ten years ago possess these things. Can the new nuclear powers afford such gambles for ten years hence with only the public sector of knowledge on which to judge? In any case, no middle power planning to go into nuclear weapons without a great power patron can hope to have a good tactical warning system in 1970 or 1980 if these are going to depend on heavy satellites and other and expensive technologies. This prospect is made even more discouraging by the fact that military rocketry is now diverging from the sort of rockets needed for space programmes.

One of the most persistent fears of the power which is starting to freeze its designs of weapons and delivery systems for operational deployment 5, 10 or 15 years from now is the likelihood of progress in defensive weapons. General staffs must take the best informed risks they can on the date of arrival and effectiveness of anti-missile missiles, the benefits which electronic counter-measures will confer on them, and the accuracy and simplicity which are available from the use of new methods. A small country embarking on its own weapons programme would be multiplying its own intelligence problem many times if it did not have the co-operation of a major power. The latest and best thought about the future of weapons could probably not be obtained with any sort of intelligence methods, and really demands a right of entry to highly classified material in either Moscow or Washington.

Thus a nation without both a substantial technology and the intimate trust of a great power will have great obstacles to overcome before it can hope to make itself a nuclear power in any genuine sense.

Other Allied Arrangements

There are certain circumstances in which powerful nations may make arrangements with their allies which will endow them with some of the attributes of nuclear power, though not with the right to exercise this power autonomously. These deserve separate consideration, if only because they are likely to increase in scope as alliances grow closer and defence arrangements become more interdependent.

The only power to have made public arrangements of this kind is the United States. Since it was decided under the NATO five year plan of 1957 that NATO forces in Europe should be equipped with both nuclear and conventional capacity, the United States has been providing her European allies with everything necessary for the delivery of nuclear weapons except the warheads themselves. This has been done by direct bilateral dealing with Britain and through the NATO organisation with other European countries and Canada.

Since these arrangements involve putting nuclear delivery systems into the possession and control of the allied country, they could theoretically provide the delivery system for a national force. This would be most difficult to achieve with single-purpose weapons closely tied to American warheads. The *Thor* and *Jupiter* ballistic missiles are the leading cases of these. The agreements which put *Thor* in England and *Jupiter* in Italy do not extend to licences revealing all the details of their construction; and it would be a clear breach of the spirit of the agreement, if not the letter, to try to use them with domestic warheads. In spite of the British anxiety to maintain a wholly national deterrent force, there has been no suggestion that the sixty *Thors* owned, manned and operated by the R.A.F. since 1958 should be carriers of anything but their American controlled warheads. The same may be said of the *Mace*, *Nike Hercules*, *Corporal* and *Honest John* missiles which the United States has supplied to a number of European countries. Weapons such as bombers which are not tied to a particular warhead would obviously be of more interest to an embryo nuclear power. The thousand odd F–104G *Starfighters* which are being built in Canada and Europe (as well as in Japan) under U.S. licence would make a good supersonic striking force over short to medium ranges.

Apart from the possible diversion of a delivery system from its American warhead to a national warhead, there are other considerations which should at least be recognised. Is it entirely inconceivable that control of the nuclear warheads for these weapons might pass into the hands of the host nation, thus suddenly and immediately creating a new nuclear power? The method used to control the *Thor* missiles in Britain, for example, is the permanent presence of a United States officer who must insert a key into the control panel to enable the count-down to go beyond a certain point. It is not known in what circumstances the warheads are attached, but the reaction time is greatly extended when they are not; so it must be assumed that in times of tension, at least, only the key carried by the U.S. officer is needed to complete the firing. He could presumably be overpowered or suborned or the physical system of controls might be tampered with. Such a misuse of the weapons would require a determined resolution on a course of action amounting to aggression against the United States and it is hard to see how relations between the British and American Governments could ever reach such a state. But in considering how powers might obtain nuclear weapons, such physical facts should at least be kept in mind. They show that there is an element of trust in the American arrangements with her allies.

The case of tactical nuclear weapons in the German Federal Republic is in some ways a special one. The large nuclear stockpiles maintained by the United States forces in Germany are for the provision of all the allied forces on the Central Front. Here there are the same possibilities of seizure, though these are perhaps modified by the presence in Germany of 250,000 American troops.

Another possibility is that the United States President might decide to release these weapons to the NATO allies. Such an act of nuclear sharing could be almost instantaneous, since the recipients possess the delivery systems, are fully ready to use them, and understand all the associated tactics and supply problems. An enemy could expect no warning at all. In fact, of course, the current trend of American policy is away from the creation of independent nuclear powers in this or any other way; and the chance that it might confer on Germany or any other European ally the accolade of nuclear power which it has been at such pains to refuse to all is negligible. The fact should be recognised, however, that the Soviet Union may genuinely fear that the disposition of American nuclear weapons in Europe is tantamount to the creation there of several 'pre-natal' nuclear powers. It may seek to take retaliatory measures, including some similar sharing arrangement with East Germany or other Warsaw Pact powers.

These European arrangements have produced one other problem. Countries which are anxious to avoid becoming independent nuclear powers but which have agreed to contribute forces to the common defence of an area may find themselves becoming nuclear powers *faute de mieux* by the nuclearisation of the agreed allied defence policy. Thus the Netherlands and Greece, say, are being asked by the United States, through NATO, to accept the arming of their aircraft with atomic bombs and to incorporate tactical nuclear missile battalions into their ground forces. If a Dutch pilot is training to drop an atomic bomb (even though it is kept in American hands in peacetime) on a target in Eastern Europe, it is not easy for the Netherlands to sustain the proposition that she is not a nuclear power. The concern of Canada over this problem will be described in Chapter 5. Only the two Scandinavian members of NATO, Norway and Denmark, have succeeded in insulating themselves against it by the fact that they have no responsibilities on the Central Front and have insisted that their own defence system must include no nuclear weapons. The position of such countries as Canada is made theoretically indefensible by the fact that NATO is only carrying out a unanimously agreed plan (MC–70) which any member of the alliance could have vetoed. Nevertheless, a small power in such an alliance as NATO is not in practice likely to exercise a veto without substantial support from others.

The fact that the possibilities outlined in this section are remote does not entitle the existing nuclear powers to ignore their implications. The purpose of drawing attention to them is to illustrate how international agreements for the disposition of these weapons on foreign military bases, however necessary they may be militarily, may have the effect of diffusing some of the attributes of nuclear power to a wider circle of countries.

PART II
Nine Leading Cases

Chapter 3

Britain

BEFORE examining the situation in those countries which are most able to build a nuclear weapons system but have not yet done so, it may be of value to study the British and French cases. These two countries are interesting for the light they shed on two different eras—that of 1945–55 when the British were taking their decisions about their bomb and its delivery system, and that of 1955–60 when the French debated about their bomb and its carrier.

The notable thing about the British Government's decision to become a nuclear power is that it does not seem to have been a decision at all. It was discovered with a certain sense of shock after the end of the Second World War that what the British regarded as the common achievement of the Manhattan Project had become a highly classified and exclusively American property. This had an important part in the apparently unanimous reaction among those concerned with such questions that Britain should make her own atomic weapons. Debate about the wisdom or value of possessing nuclear weapons did not start for about ten years.

The belief of British scientists that an atomic explosive could be designed and built went back to 1940. Without entering into the debate about who was really responsible for the war-time decision to attempt to make an atomic bomb, there is no doubt that the British Government decided at an early date that it should put a major effort into this new form of explosive. Its scientific support rested not only on the major part which British physicists had played in the exploration of the nucleus but included such men as Peierls and Frisch, who had escaped to Britain from Germany, and Halban, Kowarski and others who had escaped from France. In the course of 1941, the British and American teams working on the problem both

reached the firm conclusion that the bomb could be done
(though they were not then sure which method would be best).
The British Government decided that there was every reason
for moving the whole project across the Atlantic: the United
States had the resources, Canada would be taking an important part, and there were the dangers of bombing and possibly
invasion in Britain. There was also the simple desire to avoid
duplication.

The situation was put on a firm basis by an agreement
signed by Roosevelt and Churchill on August 19th, 1943, at
the Citadel in Quebec. It said:

Whereas it is vital to our common safety in the present war
to bring the Tube Alloys project to fruition at the earliest
moment; and whereas this may be more speedily achieved
if all available British and American brains and resources
are pooled; and whereas owing to war conditions it would
be an improvident use of war resources to duplicate plants
on a large scale on both sides of the Atlantic and therefore a
far greater expense has fallen upon the United States;

It is agreed between us

First, that we will never use this agency against each other.

Secondly, that we will not use it against third parties
without each other's consent.

Thirdly, that we will not either of us communicate any information about Tube Alloys to third parties except by
mutual consent.

Fourthly, that in view of the heavy burden of production
falling upon the United States as the result of a wise division
of war effort, the British Government recognize that any
post-war advantages of an industrial or commercial character shall be dealt with as between the United States and
Great Britain on terms to be specified by the President of
the United States to the Prime Minister of Great Britain.
The Prime Minister expressly disclaims any interest in these
industrial and commercial aspects beyond what may be
considered by the President of the United States to be fair
and just and in harmony with the economic welfare of the
world.

And Fifthly, that the following arrangements shall be made to ensure full and effective collaboration between the two countries in bringing the project to fruition:

(a) There shall be set up in Washington a Combined Policy Committee.[1] The functions of this Committee, subject to the control of the respective Governments, will be:

(1) To agree from time to time upon the programme of work to be carried out in the two countries.

(2) To keep all sections of the project under constant review.

(3) To allocate materials, apparatus and plant, in limited supply, in accordance with the requirements of the programme agreed by the Committee.

(4) To settle any questions which may arise on the interpretation or application of this Agreement.

(b) There shall be a complete interchange of information and ideas on all sections of the project between members of the Policy Committee and their immediate technical advisers.

(c) In the field of scientific research and development there shall be full and effective interchange of information and ideas between those in the two countries engaged in the same sections of the field.

(d) In the field of design, construction and operation of large-scale plants, interchange of information and ideas shall be regulated by such *ad hoc* arrangements as may, in each section of the field, appear to be necessary or desirable if the project is to be brought to fruition at the earliest moment. Such *ad hoc* arrangements shall be subject to the approval of the Policy Committee.[2]

Whether or not it was President Roosevelt's intention that the programme should be fully shared in all its military

[1] The members were the Secretary of War, Dr. Vannevar Bush and Dr. James Conant (U.S.), Field Marshal Sir John Dill and Colonel J. J. Llewellin (U.K.) and Mr. C. D. Howe (Canada).

[2] 'Articles of Agreement governing collaboration between the authorities of the U.S.A. and the U.K. in the matter of Tube Alloys (Atom Bomb Research and Development),' published April, 1954, Cmd. 9123.

implications, this was certainly the British Government's understanding. An exchange in the House of Commons in 1951—when Mr. Attlee was Prime Minister and Mr. Churchill was leader of the Opposition—shows the attitude of these two men, who had been Prime Minister and Deputy Prime Minister in 1943:

MR. CHURCHILL: Another subject of grave complaint is the inability of the Government to produce any atomic bombs of our own in the five and a half years which have passed since the war. When we remember how far we were ahead, and how we were able to deal on equal terms with the United States, it is indeed depressing to feel that we have been out-stripped by the Soviets in this field . . .

MR. ATTLEE: The right hon. Gentleman really ought not to mislead the country on a matter like this. He knows perfectly well it was by his agreement, and the agreement of the Government of which I was a Member, that the development of the atomic bomb and the making and everything took place across the other side of the Atlantic, and it is utterly untrue to suggest there has been a failure to develop it here. It is entirely wrong of him.

MR. CHURCHILL: At the end of the war we resumed full freedom to make the atomic bomb ourselves. The only reason we did not make it during the war was that we were under air bombardment. We had not got a safe place here and the United States had the facility and the credit of making it.[1]

The fact had to be faced, however, that when the war ended, the British found themselves without any share in the project. There is no doubt that the U.S. Atomic Energy Act of 1946 surprised the British government. The spy trials starting with Dr. Nunn May and leading to the *cause célèbre* of Dr. Klaus Fuchs in 1950 confirmed Congressional suspicion of British security and did much to convince the British Cabinet that no co-operation was likely in these matters for at least ten years. For some years, no one was at all clear what part nuclear

[1] *Hansard*, February 15th, 1951, columns 632–3.

weapons would take in the future of warfare: but it was quite obvious that they were an important subject for the research and development of a great power. It should be noted that in the post-war period the British armed forces built their own equipment over a very wide field, equalled only by the Soviet Union and the United States. Britain's population and wealth might appear to be of a distinctly different order from those of the United States or the Soviet Union, but the British were developing their own tanks, artillery, jet engines, bombers, fighters, transport aircraft, destroyers, aircraft carriers, and so on. The national weapons base was, and still largely is, that of a great power; and in this context a decision not to proceed with nuclear weapons would have been surprising in the post-war period.

Both in government and within public opinion, there was considerable support for military spending on research and development rather than production of what appeared to be obsolete equipment. In a country which is preoccupied with economic expansion rather than the imminent prospect of war, advanced technologies are much more attractive than expenditure on the ironmongery of conventional troops. The point was made by Mr. A. V. Alexander, the Minister of Defence, in 1947: 'I should like to refer once more to the special importance which the Government attaches to research and development, on which the Admiralty and Ministry of Supply expect to spend more than £60 million during the coming financial year.'[1] They were going ahead with stimulating research in 'the fundamentally new fields which scientific discoveries have opened up' and he was glad to note that this policy commanded universal support.

The first step in the British nuclear weapons programme was the foundation of the Atomic Energy Research Establishment at Harwell where the GLEEP reactor went critical in August 1947. Work started a month later on the first Windscale reactor for this purpose and this went critical in July, 1950. The first fission bomb was tested on October 3, 1952. The broad base of the British nuclear weapons programme is indicated by the explosion of a thermonuclear bomb in

[1] *Hansard*, March 20th, 1947, column 599.

S.N.W.–F

1957, and that from the beginning steps were taken to manufacture fissile uranium in a diffusion plant.

There was no debate or criticism of this programme, if only because Parliament and the public were unaware of it. Defence White Papers were general documents in this period in which very little information was published. Even in 1950, Mr. Emmanuel Shinwell, the Minister of Defence, had only this to say:[1]

> We cannot, and do not, ignore in our defence planning the appearance of this new and terrible weapon nor its more deadly development, the hydrogen bomb. . . . We ourselves, within the resources which we can allot to the task, are following our own programme.
>
> But no one can contemplate this activity without the most sombre apprehensions as to where it may lead. Yet no solution lies in refusing to face the facts or in failure to measure up to the probabilities of the situation. I can, therefore, assure the House that the Chiefs of Staff in their strategic planning are giving full weight to this new military factor. Beyond that I cannot go today.

When the programme had finally been made public in 1952, prior to the first test, the former Prime Minister, Mr. Attlee, explained their silence. Mr. Churchill, he said

> . . . always went about saying, 'You have done nothing about the atom bomb.' He could have informed himself fully on that had he liked, but it is much easier not to know and just to talk. Then, when it turns out that we are to have the testing of an atom bomb, the right hon. Gentleman says, 'Why did you not tell us?' Because the right hon. Gentleman never asked.
>
> MR. CHURCHILL: What I asked was, 'Why did you not convey this decision to Parliament?'
>
> MR. ATTLEE: Because I followed the course that had been laid down by the right hon. Gentleman when he was Prime Minister. It was the advice of everyone that we do not tell all these details.

[1] *Hansard*, March 16th, 1950, column 1275.

MR. CHURCHILL: That is in wartime.
MR. ATTLEE: Oh no. It was carried on after that.

In 1951 the Conservatives were returned to power. After a period of office, Mr. Churchill proclaimed himself satisfied with the vigour of his political opponents in their approach to the bomb. 'Owing to the breakdown in the exchange of information between us and the United States since 1946,' he said in 1955, 'we have had to start again independently on our own. Fortunately, executive action was taken promptly by Mr. Attlee to reduce as far as possible the delay in our nuclear development and production. By his initiative we have made our own atomic bombs.'[1] At this time he announced that work would begin on a hydrogen bomb and one was tested at Christmas Island in May 1957.

Thinking began at an early stage about the place of atomic weapons in British military doctrine—and, indeed, about why Britain wanted nuclear weapons at all. From 1947 to 1962 it is possible to trace the continuing conviction that only atomic weapons offered the hope of a serious defence at a price which the British Government could afford. In 1947, Britain had a large area of Germany to administer and a heavy responsibility with the United States, for the defence of western Europe: she still ruled India and had a major base at Suez from which her influence was applied throughout the Middle East; her military and naval commitments were spread around the world to colonial and Commonwealth territories; and her economic position was weak. Even with continued conscription and a high rate of military spending (which was imposed), her commitments seemed appalling. Had their linguistic habits been suited to it, the British would have undoubtedly been responsible for the phrase 'more bang for the buck'. The 1947 Defence White Paper made the same point at greater length:

The research and development programmes of the Admiralty and the Ministry of Supply for the financial year 1947–48 provide for expansion of effort in fundamental

[1] *Hansard*, March 1st, 1955, column 1898.

research in entirely new fields. . . . It needs no further emphasis at this time that His Majesty's Government attach the highest importance to the encouragement of scientific research and development, which is of particular relevance at a time when economic considerations must limit expenditure on new equipment so severely, and so make it more than ever essential that maximum value for money is obtained.[1]

This reason has come to influence official British doctrine in favour of a nuclear strategy, at least in Western Europe where a conventional strategy would involve a heavy national commitment. Although this is the 1962 version of the problem, in earlier years nuclear weapons had not taken on the character of absolute weapons. They were seen as a possible choice and the one which in the circumstances best suited Britain. So while many countries are now deterred from building nuclear weapons by their cost, the British were (and still are) deterred from the conventional strategy to which their instincts might lead them by a fear of what this might cost. Mr. Attlee spoke in 1955[2] of how Britain could not afford 'an immense mass of so-called conventional arms'. For a considerable time in the middle-1950s, it was being asked what use conventional weapons of any kind would be to the country.

Another reason for nuclear weapons which was taken seriously at one time was the place of Britain in the strategic targeting arrangements of the western alliance. Until about 1956, it was believed that a 'broken back war' would succeed a nuclear exchange and that the number of people who would survive would depend, at least in part, on the success of the Anglo-American striking forces in hitting targets of particular importance to the United Kingdom and its sea supplies. In the early 1950s, this argument was used to explain why a specifically British force was urgently necessary. It would hit targets of first priority to Britain but only second or third priority to the United States. Later this was expanded to a purely numerical argument by Mr. Churchill: 'Should war come, which God

[1] 'Statement Relating to Defence', February 1947.
[2] *Hansard*, March 2nd, 1955, column 2178.

forbid, there are a large number of targets that we and the Americans must be able to strike at once. There are scores of airfields from which the Soviets could launch attacks with hydrogen bombs as soon as they have the bombers to carry them. It is essential to our deterrent policy and to our survival to have, with our American Allies, the strength and numbers to be able to paralyse these potential Communist assaults in the first few hours of the war, should it come.'[1] Mr. Harold Macmillan, who was then Minister of Defence, said that for Britain the doctrine of leaving nuclear weapons to the United States 'surrenders our power to influence American policy and then, stategically and tactically, it equally deprives us of any influence over the selection of targets and use of our vital striking forces.'

The reasoning of the annual White Papers may be traced. The 1955 Defence White Paper said that the nation's duty was to build up its forces with those of its allies into 'the most powerful deterrent we can achieve'. That in 1956 said that British forces must make 'a contribution to the Allied deterrent commensurate with our standing as a world power.' That in 1957 found a wide measure of agreement that Britain 'must possess an appreciable element of nuclear deterrent power of her own.' In 1958, it was stated that when fully equipped with megaton weapons the British bomber force 'will in itself constitute a formidable deterrent.' This stirred up so much debate that nothing was said in 1959 and the tone in 1960 was rather different: 'The V-bomber force remains the United Kingdom's main contribution to the strategic nuclear power of the West.' In 1961, it was said that the Government believed it to be in the national interest that it should continue to share the burden and responsibility of maintaining this important element in the total power of the Western deterrent.' That White Paper also contained a new tactical argument for a British share. It said that the British forced increased dispersal and reduced reaction time. The argument is that bombers in Britain can hit Russian targets much faster than those in the U.S. and so can be of special value in retaliation.

---

[1] *Hansard*, March 1st, 1955, columns 1900–1.

Another main line of argument over the years has been that a specifically British force increased credibility. This really owes its origin to the fear of a renewal of American isolationism which lay behind the general British policy of self-sufficiency in weapons after 1945. Mr. Attlee said in 1952: 'I do not believe it is right that this country should be absolutely dependent on the United States of America. That is one very good reason for going ahead with our own work on the atomic bomb.'[1] The idea that Britain would use nuclear weapons in Europe when the United States might be unwilling to do so has not stood up to the experience of the intervening years. Nevertheless, the argument that situations always develop differently from what was expected carries weight with military planners and it is felt that Britain will obviously be much more ready to use nuclear weapons, at least in defence of the British Isles. Some opinion also feels that the bomber force offers a certain backing to Commonwealth countries which the United States might be less willing to extend; and Britain has undertaken military interdiction commitments to the Central Treaty Organisation (the former Bagdad Pact) of which the United States is still not formally a member.

Finally, there is the all-important issue of influence. It is argued that Britain will have more say in Washington because, being an atomic power, she is a more important power. Although this has been seriously questioned, Mr. Attlee, for one, was in no doubt about it. In 1955, he said: 'I think that we have influence in the world. That influence does not depend solely upon the possession of weapons, although I have found, in practical conversations, that the fact that we do possess these weapons does have an effect upon the rulers of other countries. It is quite an illusion to think that it does not have an effect.'[2] Another aspect of influence concerns disarmament. Many of those in Britain who abhorred nuclear weapons were undoubtedly influenced by the suggestion that their country's efforts for disarmament were made more effective by her membership in the nuclear club. In recent years, the nuclear tests conference in Geneva has had the character of

[1] *Hansard*, March 5th, 1952, column 537.
[2] *Hansard*, March 2nd, 1955, column 2179.

a club meeting. The Defence White Paper of 1961 said that the British nuclear force 'also substantially increases our influence in negotiations for a nuclear test agreement, disarmament, and the reorganization of NATO strategy.'

The British nuclear weapons force has always been primarily strategic with the main Soviet cities within range as its primary targets. In official Air Staff thinking, it took over where the mass bombing of Germany by Bomber Command left off. To provide a carrier for the coming bomb, the Royal Air Force put out a requirement on January 1, 1947, for a bomber which was later officially said to be two and a half to three times more effective than contemporary bombers in altitude, speed and range. Two aircraft were developed and ordered to this specification—the Avro *Vulcan* and the Handley Page *Victor*—and their performance suggests that the requirement was for an aircraft able to fly at 50,000 feet and 600 m.p.h. In case neither of these advanced swept-wing aircraft succeeded (or they came too late), a less ambitious type, the Vickers *Valiant*, was also ordered and went into squadron service in January 1955. *Vulcans* went into squadron service in July, 1957, and the *Victors* in the Spring of 1958. Mark 2 *Vulcans* and *Victors* were designed to carry the Avro *Blue Steel* stand-off bomb, which is due in service late in 1962. The Mark 2 *Vulcans* are expected to become carriers for the American *Skybolt* airborne ballistic missile (with British-built warheads) in 1965. A proportion of the *Valiants* have become refuelling tankers and others have been committed to NATO. Some *Victors* operate in the photographic reconnaissance role and presumably some carry electronic counter-measures to help bombers to penetrate radar screens undetected and to jam the radio and radar of attacking fighters and missiles. The total cost of this force was about £500 million.

The aim of the V-bomber force has apparently been a front line between 150 and 200 aircraft and their crews have reached very high standards of efficiency. Concern about the vulnerability of a bomber force developed in the Royal Air Force at the same time as it developed in the United States Air Force—in 1958. Two major measures were taken to deal with this problem. A system of dispersal airfields was developed with

enough to take the entire force in groups of four. This was the
number which it was thought could be got off a single runway
in less than four minutes. The other measure was the development of a simultaneous starter for the four engines which
radically reduced the time needed for running up. In fact, the
squadrons have managed through operational improvements
to get all four into the air in less than two minutes from the
time they reach their cockpits.

A fourth strategic bomber, designated the Avro 730, was
being designed as a supersonic successor to the V-bombers but
was cancelled in 1957 when it was decided that the future of
heavy nuclear forces lay in ballistic missiles. At that time, the
foundations for the British liquid-fuelled rocket *Blue Streak* had
been laid through the agreements to produce an American
rocket engine and guidance system under licence and the
development of a re-entry research rocket, *Black Knight*. In
1958, it was revealed that a British ballistic rocket was being
developed 'on the highest priority, in close co-operation with
the United States.' Work on this continued until 1960 when it
was cancelled as a military project though continuing as a
primary space booster.

The reasons for the cancellation of *Blue Streak* were both
political and technical. For some years the Royal Navy had
been taking a serious interest in the prospect of a submarine-
based missile. Because of their major effort on the *Polaris* system, the United States Navy suggested that Britain should not
undertake separate development but should attach a team to
the *Polaris* project. The growing success of this system gave
serious concern to the Royal Air Force, which was heavily
committed to its role as the service responsible for delivering
the deterrent. It gave its full support to *Blue Streak* partly, no
doubt, to avoid the adoption of a naval weapon, and *Blue
Streak* also enjoyed the loyalty of the Ministry of Defence. In
1959, the Minister of Defence, Mr. Sandys, decided that since
the full deployment of *Blue Streak* on underground bases from
1965 on would cost about £600 millions it would be too expensive merely to supplement the V-force and would have to replace it. In other words, the R.A.F. would lose its medium
bomber force and become ground-based nuclear artillery.

R.A.F. loyalty to *Blue Streak* rapidly disappeared. At the same time, the United States Air Force was having remarkable success with its test programme for an air-launched ballistic missile and had decided that this would be feasible. The R.A.F. took it up enthusiastically for the V-bombers. *Blue Streak* by then already belonged to a technically outdated generation—the generation of the *Atlas*, *Titan* and *Jupiter* liquid-fuelled missiles which were being severely cut back in the United States—and the expensive programme for deployment after 1965 found itself with neither technical nor service support. In his meetings with President Eisenhower in early 1960, Mr. Macmillan, the Prime Minister, obtained agreement in principle to the purchase of *Skybolt* in 1965 and *Polaris*, if desired, in 1970.

Politically, the British nuclear force began to encounter strong opposition almost as soon as it became known fully to the public. Although represented only by a small minority among Labour Members of Parliament and unrepresented in the Conservative Party, the Campaign for Nuclear Disarmament and its various off-shoots became a lively force in the political life of the country from 1957 on. The Labour Party Conference adopted a resolution sponsored by CND supporters in 1960, though this was rejected by the Parliamentary Party and reversed in 1961. The notion that Britain should give a lead by scrapping her own nuclear weapons made a strong appeal to radicals and the idea of a non-nuclear club gained general support outside the Conservative Party in the 1959–60 period. This was a suggestion that Britain should renounce her own nuclear weapons if the leading non-nuclear powers (presumably led by France and China) would forswear them. This would leave the United States and Soviet Union with nuclear deterrents on behalf of themselves and their allies. The Labour Party gave official support to this proposal. The Labour Party also went a long way towards meeting the demand for unilateral nuclear disarmament among its supporters by arguing that *Skybolt* was largely imaginary (or, alternatively, that the American Government would not allow it to be sold to the R.A.F.) and that no successor should be created to the V-bomber force. Tactical

nuclear weapons in NATO should remain a U.S. responsibility. Thus Britain as a nuclear power would erode away. The
reason, however, would not be an objection in principle to
nuclear weapons but merely an inevitable technical trend.
The party leadership's offer to grant on technical grounds
what the disarmers wanted as a matter of principle merely
served to exacerbate the argument.

The cancellation of *Blue Streak* made a considerable impact
on the public mind. It was widely felt that the country had
over-reached itself by going into sophisticated rockets. The
degree of American co-operation in the weapon was never
publicly known and the great expense for little deployment in
the equivalent American weapons was never recognised. In the
press and much public opinion, there was a feeling that this
marked the end of an era of going it alone and pressure grew
for a reduction of the nuclear weapons effort and an increase
in the British contribution to ground forces in Europe. The
Government's reply to this was that it had been spending less
than 10 per cent of the defence budget on the bomber force,
its bombs and related research and development. A particularly strong attack on the whole strategic deterrent policy was
made during the 1961 defence debate in the House of Commons by Mr. Aubrey Jones, a Conservative who had been
Minister of Supply from 1957 to 1959. He said: 'I am driven
to the conclusion that within a few years from now any talk
about the desirability of this country's making an independent
contribution to the nuclear deterrent will be purely and
utterly theoretical. I think that we are face to face with the
plain fact that once the *Blue Streak* weapon had gone this
country ceased to be able to develop and manufacture a
deterrent weapon which was up to date.' Much intelligent
public opinion felt in 1962 that a withdrawal from heavy
nuclear weapons was inevitable, but there is no evidence that
this was the official view. Service thinking for the future concentrated on the force after 1970 and both nuclear submarines
(which Britain is building as anti-submarine weapons) and
aircraft able to stand an air alert were actively considered.
There was interest in the Super VC-10 airliner and an aircraft
using variable sweep adapted for a later *Skybolt*. The Ministry

of Defence was also interested in the TSR-2 supersonic low-level bomber as a possible strategic weapon.

The future in Britain will certainly be one of continuing debate. As a country which has sought to make an important contribution to the Western alliance through a heavy nuclear force it has undoubtedly been disillusioned. Two things have made this contribution less impressive to her allies, and especially to the United States: the fact that nuclear weapons have not fulfilled the promise that they would invariably be the most effective weapons of defence because they so often cannot be used; and the fact that they suddenly, in the mid-fifties, became plentiful. The NATO, CENTO and SEATO alliances have requirements for conventional fire-power which are never likely to be met while in nuclear weapons it is widely felt that they are saturated. As a result, the V-bomber force has not been as gratefully received as its sponsors hoped. Rightly or wrongly, this means that it is yielding less benefit inside the Atlantic Alliance—and especially in Washington—than a greater conventional effort might have done. Indeed there has been a persistent tendency in Washington to suggest that the force was ineffectual—though this view is seldom expressed by the Strategic Air Command. It is notable that when the retaliatory power of the United States is discussed by Congressional committees Bomber Command's possible share is not mentioned. The defence of Germany would never be mentioned without a description of the German, British, French, Belgian, Dutch and Canadian shares.

Inside Britain itself, there was undoubtedly profound discomfort at the thought that the national example might have been the signal for the middle powers to go into nuclear weapons. The French bomb and the general sense that this will go on have in a sense by-passed this: Britain is no longer alone outside the two giants in demanding these weapons. Nevertheless, the unlikelihood of American isolation (a real danger to be insured against in 1946), the atmosphere of nuclear plenty and conventional poverty, and the proposed introduction of major American-built missiles into the British retaliatory force have all reduced the incentives. It may be doubted whether a British Government in the near future would agree to give up a particular category of weapons outside the context of an East-West disarmament agreement. But the nuclear force is already extensively integrated into S.A.C. and will undoubtedly move with national policy towards an increasing unity in the North Atlantic area.

Chapter 4

France

FRANCE stands today as the leading example for any country planning to produce nuclear weapons. She is the only one of the four nuclear powers which did not start seriously until well after the end of the Second World War; she had a full public debate in which the need for an effective delivery system was recognised as the main hurdle; she has shown publicly the inevitable tension between strengthening influence with a great power ally and laying the foundations for an independent foreign policy; and she has conducted a major debate on the reasons for possessing nuclear weapons.

French scientists took a prominent part in the international effort which led ultimately to the release of atomic power in military weapons. Joliot-Curie, Halban and Kowarski were among those who, before 1940, were showing that nuclear fission resulted in an emission of neutrons which could lead to a chain reaction. Halban and Kowarski went to Britain after the fall of France and then to Canada where they were joined by Auger, Goldschmidt and Guéron. These men formed the basis of the Commissariat à l'energie atomique (C.E.A.) which was created after the war. This expanded steadily until in 1952 it employed 1,800 people and had a budget sufficient to develop the basic nuclear technology of the country. Uranium deposits exist inside France herself and in 1946 a plant was built near Corbeil, south of Paris, which has since maintained a supply of natural uranium to French atomic piles.

The C.E.A. built its first research laboratories at Chatillon and in 1948 a pile called Zoe began operation. A much larger research centre then followed at Saclay with particle accelerators and a pressurised gas reactor (the first anywhere) known as EL-2. It was at this stage (1952) that the first five year plan for French atomic development was worked out and put into operation with an original budget of 40,000m. old francs (about £40m.) which was raised to 100,000m. old francs (about £100m.) in 1955. From this time on, there was a consistent progress towards a nuclear weapons programme which was remarkably independent of changing governments and even of occasional political decisions, or apparent decisions, not to produce a French bomb.

The greatest effort went into the Marcoule centre, where the G-1 reactor began operation in 1956, giving 40,000 thermal kW. and (ultimately) one kilogram of plutonium a month. This plutonium was not available until 1958 at about the same time as the G-2 reactor (which was three times as large as G-1) became critical. G-2 reached full power in the spring of 1959. Each of these stages involved the government in an increasing level of expenditure and a more conscious decision to proceed with nuclear weapons. On the other hand, each time the issue was presented it was possible to suggest that there was no need to take the decision to build a bomb. Until 1959, ministers who did not like the idea particularly were able to suggest that they were not committed to nuclear weapons. Each major decision seems to have gone in the direction which a bomb programme would have indicated, but this does not prove that there were not good non-military reasons. In 1950, it is recorded,[1] a meeting was held at Saclay attended by Joliot-Curie, Dautry, Goldschmidt, Guéron, Kowarski, Perrin, Rocard and Leprince-Ringuet at which Kowarski advocated a programme of research reactors and Goldschmidt argued that power reactors were needed to produce plutonium. The Goldschmidt policy was adopted. While it was possible to argue that a substantial supply of plutonium would be valuable to the country for many purposes, all these men would know that they were creating the option on a bomb. This issue came to a head once more over the 80,000 million old francs needed for the G-3 addition to Marcoule, which was designed to bring the output of Marcoule up to 800

[1] This is described by M. Nicholas Vichney: *Le Monde*, December 31st, 1959.

tons of uranium a year by 1959. The decision to grant the
necessary money to M. Gaston Palewski early in 1955 had the
clearest military implications. So, too, had the creation of the
Comité des explosifs nucléaires (C.E.N.), a military group
which was attached to the C.E.A. Although this took place
under the government of M. Mendès-France (later a strong
critic of the *force de frappe*), it should be noted that his Minister
of Defence was General Koenig, a Gaullist[1]. This was only a
few months after M. Pleven, who had been Minister of
Defence, had said: 'Our military research in atomic matters
cannot yet be allotted as large amounts as might be wished. I
think that in the coming months and certainly before the
preparation of the 1955 budget the Government will have to
examine in detail the problems involved in a country of
France's importance manufacturing nuclear weapons.' An
examination of the accompanying chart[2] will show why this
was the case and how the rapidly rising graph of the previous
two years is likely to force governments to really serious study
of the financial implications six or seven years after they begin
their nuclear research programme.

As late as April, 1955, prominent politicians were saying
that the French atomic programme was entirely peaceful. M.
Faure, who was then Prime Minister of France, said at a press
conference on April 13 that the Government had decided 'to
eliminate research devoted to specifically military uses [of
atomic energy]. Consequently we do not intend to devote any
study to the creation of an H-bomb or any other bomb.' He
said at the same time that France must make rapid progress
towards atomic power and was even in favour of atomic propulsion systems. One must conclude that the programme
which he was financing at that time—the money for G-3 was
being voted—had been presented to him as one which could
at least enjoy the option of peaceful use. This is suggested by
the statement of M. Pflimlin, who was Minister of Finance,
that he hoped they would soon possess atomic centres and

---

[1] An excellent discussion of the political background to the
French bomb by George A. Kelly is contained in the Fall, 1960,
issue of *Orbis*.
[2] Chart 1, page 93.

atomically-propelled ships. 'On the other hand I hope that we shall not build atomic bombs.'[1]

In 1956, three things came together to force the politicians to come to terms with the real situation which was developing under their authority: the formation of the Republican Front Government led by the Socialist leader, M. Guy Mollet; the erosion of the Geneva spirit which had obliged all public men to keep their military activities modestly in the background; and the Euratom Treaty which brought the future purposes of all the subscribing countries into the open. M. Mollet came to power with the firmest anti-nuclear views. In his investiture speech, he said that his government was pledged to the use of fissile material 'for exclusively peaceful purposes' and expressed strong support for Euratom. Since 'anyone who possesses nuclear material is capable of making atomic bombs', the French Government wanted Euratom to have exclusive rights to all nuclear materials: and it did not want to have bombs manufactured on a European basis. The Euratom Treaty originally contained a provision obliging any member to obtain the agreement of half the members for any military nuclear activities; but a compromise was worked out in which the French agreed merely not to conduct tests for four years. This compromise was obviously accompanied by tacit agreement to leave the French to their national programme since M. Bourgès-Maunoury, the Minister of Defence, was able to say in the debate that France had to choose between the possession of nuclear weapons and the abandonment of her national defence. This statement reflected the views of the armed forces and the Gaullists, which had been put with increasing force in the preceding years. The fact that the Gaullists voted for the Euratom Treaty was proof enough that the assurances of the government and their partners to the treaty were unambiguous.

The debate about the right policy for France then began in earnest and continued to grow until 1960 when French tests began and the five-year plan for a *force de frappe* was passed into law. Marshal Juin, whose authority was very great with the

[1] Interview published in *Nouvel Alsacien*, quoted in *Orbis*, Fall, 1960, p. 290.

army and the country, said at Lausanne in February, 1958, that 'if France had the atom bomb her rights would not be disputed'. This was a good reflection of military opinion in that period which for a number of reasons had been building up in favour of atomic weapons. It should be remembered that this was the time of the greatest concentration on nuclear weapons in Western policy. NATO was putting the MC-70 plan into effect to give it the option of fighting with or without nuclear weapons but with a strong emphasis on the impossibility of accepting any serious aggression in Europe without using them; Britain was hoping to achieve substantial reductions in her defence spending by reducing her conventional forces in the light of her growing nuclear strength; and American theorists, such as Henry Kissinger, were reflecting an official line which renounced the nuclear abstention of the Korean War in all but the smallest situations. Such French thinkers as General Gallois and General Carpentier became identified with the view that the American nuclear presence in Europe was bound to become less credible as the Russian long-range striking force obtained an unchallenged ability to hit at the United States. The British nuclear weapons force was thought by them to be no more reliable in defending France. A French force, even if small, would leave no doubt in the minds of the Russians that any attempt to invade Western Europe would mean nuclear war. As the prize was relatively small, the deterrent could be relatively small. To this was added the more conventional argument that France's voice would only be heard in Washington when it spoke with all the force of nuclear weapons behind it.

The most noted military opponent was General Valluy, who showed great concern with the effect of a French bomb on the American alliance. A surprising synthesis of his views with those of General Gallois, General Geleé, General Nicot and M. René Massigli, the former ambassador to London, was published late in 1960 and may be regarded as the informed orthodox defence of the French position. It summarised nine considerations:

1. The international authority of nations depends on a

modern army and an effective force must have nuclear weapons.

2. Such arms discourage an aggressor by threatening him with destruction out of proportion to what he stands to gain.

3. The defence of Europe, the greatest interest of France, involves the use of nuclear weapons, at least tactically.

4. Inside the North Atlantic Alliance, the powers which manufacture nuclear weapons—the United States and Great Britain—control their use nationally or under bilateral arrangements.

5. With American cities threatened by the Russians, the guarantee which other members draw from the American atomic arsenal is no longer absolute.

6. An integrated NATO nuclear force has never been proposed. It is a first principle of the U.S. and U.K. that the control of their nuclear weapons should not be abandoned to another power and final authority would be kept in Washington if it was decided to put strategic arms symbolically under the Supreme Allied Commander.

7. A European force could only be constituted in a European defence community under a federal government in a European state. French nuclear production should not be subordinated to a situation which is not likely in the near future.

8. A French nuclear force would:

    (a) Assure national security if the system of collective security failed and would increase the global deterrent capacity of the Atlantic Alliance by increasing the credibility (*vraisemblance de l'emploi*) of a nuclear force based on the Continent.

    (b) Make closer the relations between France and the U.S. by getting rid of the impediment of nuclear secrets. France has the right to think that she will be given the same treatment as Great Britain.

    (c) Give France more authority in international negotiations and especially in the disarmament negotiations.

9. Given the limited resources of France and assuming reasonable aid from her allies, it is important to stop the

creation of a nuclear force from dangerously limiting the
modernisation of conventional forces and adapt them to
other dangers besides nuclear war. The object of the
nuclear force will not be achieved if it is at the price of
enfeebling conventional defence and the economic and
moral capacity for resistance in the nation.[1]

This broad position steadily prevailed with official opinion.
General de Gaulle's return to power removed the final ambiguities of public policy, though there had been no doubt of
the outcome since 1956.

In a speech at the Centre des Hautes Etudes Militaires on
November 3rd, 1959, the President put his intentions clearly.
He said:

The idea of a defence for France and the Community which
is a French defence—this idea ought to be fundamental to
your thinking. The conclusion is obvious: that we must discover how to provide ourselves with a force able to act on its
own account, what is usually known as a 'striking force' able
to be sent to any place at any time. It goes without saying
that the foundation of this force will be atomic armament—
whether we make it or buy it—and it must belong to us: and
since eventually it will be possible for us to be destroyed
from any point on earth, our force must be able to act anywhere on earth.

A few days later, he confirmed France's refusal to be
influenced by the moratorium on nuclear tests which the
Americans, Russians and British had declared when they had
begun their conference for the abolition of nuclear tests at
Geneva in November, 1958: 'The Russians and the Anglo-
Americans have suspended their nuclear tests, but that does
nothing to stop the menace from existing and even from growing every day, since the two rivals are keeping their nuclear
armament and manufacturing more. At present, they are
putting immense effort into providing themselves with missiles
which have far greater range and power . . . Who can say
what will happen tomorrow? One can well imagine, for
example, that on some terrible occasion, Western Europe

[1] *Le Monde*, November 12th, 1960.

might be obliterated from Moscow and Central Europe from Washington.'

This was merely the full public acceptance for the first time of a reality to which French policy had become steadily committed. The Foreign Minister, M. Couve de Murville, was not exaggerating very much when he said on December 29th, 1959, to the National Assembly that the decision had been taken five years before and had never been contested.

In spite of this, the arrival of the first nuclear device stirred up a domestic debate which had not been equalled in any of the three first nuclear powers. It was also the subject of intense international interest. It led to the overwhelming denunciation of France by the United Nations General Assembly and produced an active series of negotiations with the United States Government in which Washington showed itself unsympathetic to French policy. On balance, the first generation of French nuclear devices undoubtedly increased rather than decreased the strain in relations between the two countries.

The issue of sharing was dealt with to a large extent in 1959. M. Alphand, the French Ambassador to the United States, had been told in 1959 that no secrets would be opened merely because a few nominal bombs were let off. The French, nevertheless, were influenced to some extent by the wording of the 1958 amendment of the Atomic Energy Act as the semi-official nine-point statement showed. The Act gave the impression that it was only a matter of time until full American sharing would be forthcoming. France was certainly not going to give what she regarded as unilateral concessions and in the spring of 1959 she refused the American offer of IRBMs on French soil with the retention of the warheads under American control to meet the needs of NATO planning.

During the year after this, it became obvious that General de Gaulle had established a wider principle in these matters. He was openly refusing the soil of France to the United States for the stock-piling of tactical nuclear weapons. Agreements dated July 29th, 1959, allowed the U.S. Administration to share information on the effects and sizes of atomic weapons with West Germany, Turkey, the Netherlands and Canada, but not with France. It was not decided to extend these arrangements to France until September, 1961, at a time when France was restoring troops to European soil to meet the growing tension over Berlin.

In the middle of 1959, however, the United States Government appeared to be placing no effective limits on the sharing of essential components to delivery systems. It allowed the Pratt and Whitney aero-engine company to sign an agreement with the French firm of SNECMA for the licence production of the turbo-jet engines for the proposed *Mirage* 4B nuclear bomber. A few months later this aircraft was cancelled. It is possible that this was because of an Anglo-American decision to withhold co-operation in this field (a British engine was also available), but it seems more likely that the problem was simply one of expense. Whatever the reason, the *Mirage* 4B of 125,000 pounds take-off weight gave way to the very different *Mirage* 4A of 50,000 pounds weight. This made France the first nation to go into atomic weapons without a clear plan for a strategic nuclear delivery system against her major potential enemy. It is, of course, true that the *Mirage* 4A could mount a strike against the Soviet Union with flight refuelling and for this reason a certain number of them will be produced as tankers. Its range has generally been quoted as between 1,600 and 2,000 kilometres without refuelling. The aircraft will fly at Mach 2 (twice the speed of sound) and apparently achieves good economy at Mach 1.6. It is assumed, however, that for long range missions it would normally fly subsonically much of the way. The design incorporates a jamming system, for which there are high hopes, low-level performance at high subsonic speeds, and the possibility of adaptation to vertical take-off— presumably based on the Rolls-Royce RB-162 direct lift jet engine which the French government is developing with Britain and Germany and has applied to a development of the *Mirage 3*. General de Gaulle made a concession of the greatest importance when he agreed that the *Mirage* 4B should be cancelled. France by that act denied herself the capacity to threaten the Soviet Union seriously with nuclear retaliation on its own territory until 1970 or after. It is therefore not surprising that as soon as the Government revealed in detail its plan for the *force de frappe*, opposition based on the inadequacy of the delivery system began to grow. Together with fears that France was endangering the Atlantic Alliance, the unity of Western Europe and the American guarantee, this produced a parliamentary opposition which had to be overcome by recourse to a vote of confidence in the government.

The year 1960 was a stormy one for the French nuclear weapons programme. It began with the first test on February 13th which was followed immediately by a second on April 1st. (The third was held at the end of the year, on December 27th, and the fourth on April 25th, 1961). The Sahara range in the Reggane area had been selected for its totally deserted character and had been developed from the beginning of 1957 for testing. According to M. Perret-Gentil, who has written with authority about French tests, the first device was known as Type A and yielded the equivalent of 70 kilotons of TNT.[1] An American report put it at 79; the French let 60–70 kilotons be known. It used the obvious method of firing two sub-critical masses of plutonium together. Right from these first devices, the French weapons programme was distinguishing between different uses of weapons and designing differently for them. As Type A was to find information needed for a strategic weapon, Type B, the second one, was for tactical purposes. Its test was notable for the active participation of the three armed forces, each of which had an area around the centre of the explosion where it conducted the experiments it needed. The explosion was at ground level and is believed to have been in the 15–20 kiloton range. The hole it created was said to be several hundred metres in diameter and 50 meters deep. The third and fourth tests were, respectively, in the 5–10 kiloton range and the 2–3 kiloton range. After the fourth it was announced that future tests would be held underground until the French hydrogen device was ready.

The political effects of the first test were far more serious than those which had accompanied those of the first three nuclear powers. At that time the existing nuclear powers were in the middle of their three-year moratorium on tests which was summarily ended in August 1961, and by a vote of 51 to 16 with 15 abstentions the United Nations General Assembly

[1] *Revue Militaire Suisse*, August 1960 and January 1961.

called on France on November 20th, 1959, to refrain from the Sahara tests. The 51 included the Soviet bloc and what are usually known as the Afro-Asian bloc plus Cuba, Venezuela and Yugoslavia; and it also included Canada, Norway, Denmark and New Zealand. Most of the Latin American countries abstained as did the Australians, Greeks and Turks. France had only her five Common Market partners, the United States, Britain, Israel, Spain, Portugal, South Africa and five Latin American countries on her side. The next day, the assembly voted by 60 votes to 1 (France herself) to ask the three powers meeting at Geneva to agree to ban nuclear tests and ask others in the meanwhile to refrain from testing.

This resolution was ignored and resented in Paris and the test went ahead. When the first device went off, President de Gaulle put out this message: 'General de Gaulle expresses the thanks of the whole country to those who have made this success possible: ministers and scientists, officers and engineers, industrialists and technicians. Thus France, thanks only to her national effort, can add strength to her defences, to those of the Community, and those of the West. In addition, the Republic of France is now in a better position to exert its influence for agreement between the atomic powers with a view to achieving nuclear disarmament.'

He also sent the following message to M. Pierre Guillamaut, the Prime Minister's minister-delegate at Reggane: 'Hurrah for France! From this morning she is strong and prouder. From the bottom of my heart thanks to you and to those who have brought her this magnificent success.'

The hostile reaction of the United Nations was caused in part by the resentment of some of the African states (particularly Ghana) at the explosion of nuclear weapons on African soil. Although there were some protests at each test, these declined steadily in importance. There remained the domestic troubles and these broke out in earnest in the course of 1960. The progress of defence thinking generally had introduced the notion of vulnerability into American and British, if not Russian, planning. It was this (combined with the proof of the accuracy of Russian missiles which they showed when they orbited the moon) which led directly to the cancellation of

Blue Streak. Air defences were also seen to be improving steadily. Since in both the United States and Britain, there were severe critics of the existing delivery systems for the heavy nuclear forces it is not surprising that pressure grew for a clear statement of the French Government's intentions.

This was met with the publication of a *loi-programme*, a five year plan, on July 21st, 1960. This divided military expenditure into current and investment—the division in 1960 being 10,000m. N.F. for current maintenance and 6,000m. N.F. for investment. The *loi-programme* covered the investment portion for the five years to the end of 1964 and made this a total of 31,160m. N.F.—about £2,265m. This planned portion was to be 35 per cent of all defence spending. Of this amount, just under 20 per cent—6,000m. N.F., or £436m.—was to be spent on the construction of the *force de frappe*. (This figure is fairly close to the £500m. spent by the United Kingdom on the construction of the V-bomber force between 1950 and 1962 and the £600m. which would have been spent on the *Blue Streak* force between 1955 and 1965). The investment spending on the *force de frappe* will therefore probably be between 7 and 8 per cent of the total defence budget. The break-down was as follows in millions of New Francs:

Expenditure on nuclear weapons	3,988 (£290m.)
Mirage 4 programme	1,000 (£73m.)
Ballistic missile programme	1,060 (£77m.)

The plan obtained the support of the Defence Committee of the National Assembly on October 11th by a vote of 42 to 33 after the Gaullists had asked for assurances about the maintenance of France's alliances and the modernisation of all branches of the armed forces equally. The committee asked for the transfer of 280m. N.F. from supersonic aircraft to new equipment for the army and the development of tactical nuclear weapons and 120m. N.F. from research to the construction of an experimental nuclear submarine. It was revealed that spending on the *Mirage 4* (in N.F.) would be 11m. in 1960, 64m. in 1961, 145m. in 1962, 176m. in 1963, 180m. in 1964 and 424m. after the end of the period.

The publication of these and earlier figures makes it possible to get a general idea of the trend of spending in the French atomic weapons programme (Chart 1). This shows both how cheap the early option can be and how rapidly the graph rises when it is decided to take this up.

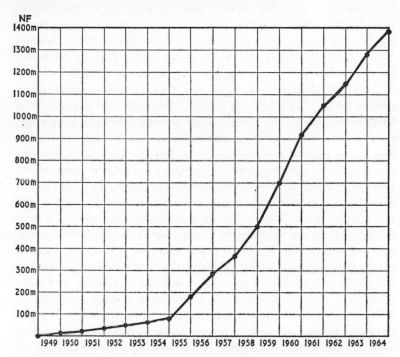

Estimated annual expenditure on the French atomic programme and *force de frappe*

A general examination of the *loi-programme* leaves no doubt that France is hoping that her first generation of weapons with their supersonic light bomber delivery system will bring American co-operation. From the earliest days, General de Gaulle has been planning a solid fuel ballistic missile to be ready for service by about 1970. In 1959, the *Société d'Etudes et de Réalisation d'Engins Balistiques* (SEREB) had been created to begin studies of an advanced delivery system. This was a combination of French companies and it immediately obtained serious interest from American firms with a view to a series of licence agreements. The parallel with the British *Blue Streak* programme was clear since co-operation in rocketry involved no alteration in the Atomic Energy Act. There was particular concern about the development of inertial guidance systems such as had been given to the British both for *Blue Streak* and (a more advanced system) the ground-to-ground bombardment weapon *Blue Water*. The Aerojet General Corporation, the leading American firm in solid fuel rocket technology, was engaged in the most detailed discussions with SEREB and with the Government-owned aero-engine firm, SNECMA. It is now generally accepted that in September, 1959, an order went out to all American companies forbidding co-operation on missile vehicle projects.[1] While the official reason for this is that the United States was encouraging Europe in the notion of a joint IRBM project and therefore would not support national projects, the real reason was the bad and worsening relations between the two countries. The United States Administration had developed a profound distrust for the French Government. Nevertheless, some aid has been given for the French nuclear submarine (which might or might not be for strategic nuclear weapons purposes) for which a land-based prototype will start running at Cadarache in 1963. Some enriched uranium has been made available, though it has apparently been refused for the sea-going versions. France should have her own enriched uranium when her isotope separation plan starts working at Pierrelatte in 1965.

In the early days of *force de frappe* thinking, the army favoured simple weapons which could be changed easily to nuclear warheads. The Air Force advocated a longer term approach and, on the whole, carried the day. References to plans to put nuclear warheads on the army's SE-4200 short-range missile (and the later 100-kilometre SE-4500) are now much less frequent. SEREB is apparently going ahead with a solid-fuelled missile with a range of 1,500–2,500 miles. Its first rocket, the solid fuel *Agate*, was fired without guidance to a height of forty miles with instruments weighing 1,650 pounds in the summer of 1961. This is presumably the beginning of a

[1] See *Aviation Week*, August 21st, 1961, p. 32.

line of rockets intended to lead to an operational weapon about
1970.

The debate on the *loi-programme* late in 1960, exposed the
French dilemma. The Prime Minister, M. Debré, began by
attacking those who thought France was damaging her
alliances. They were merely continuing an effort which had
been going on for ten years by governments which had no
intention of interfering with France's alliances. But alliances
were limited. 'There is no integration in atomic weapons, and
no-one is inclined at present to integrate deterrent forces. It is
only possible to have co-operation between states able to offer
something to a common effort.' France also had to consider
the evolution of technology and her responsibilities:

'There is no modern defence', he said, 'for those who do
not have a modern arsenal. Studies and research carried out
over a period of ten years by France put us in a position today
to start the fabrication of atomic bombs . . . We have the
right and the duty to prepare our defences so as to force a
potential aggressor to think; even more, we are responsible for
a part of European and Atlantic security and that of the young
African states who know they can count on us.'

The opposition was both technical and political. The
Socialist Party's parliamentary groups had already said that
very important resources were going into the *force de frappe*
'whose efficiency, considered within a purely national framework, is illusory'. M. Jules Moch, writing in *Le Monde* (December 6th, 1960), said that 'the thousand million new francs for
aircraft will undoubtedly be spent on pure loss, except for the
constructors. Before the 50 or 60 machines thus acquired enter
service, they "are in danger of being rapidly replaced" as
General Valluy has pointed out. . . . Bombing by aircraft
belongs to the past, even if one arms them with guided weapons which free them from the need to approach the target.'

The political objections were not to nuclear weapons, but to
the effect that the Government's programme was having on
the alliance. M. Paul Reynaud, a former Prime Minister, said
that a French nuclear striking force must lead in time to a
German one. The job should be done by an integrated Europe.
'To go into nuclear weapons research when one is a member

of an alliance of which the principal partner has a powerful atomic force is implicitly to suspect them,' he said 'it is to suspect the United States of one day abandoning her allies. For the United States to leave Europe would be the greatest betrayal in history. This suspicion is injurious and dangerous'. M. Jean-Paul David was widely applauded when he asked all the nations of Europe to pool their resources. 'A national deterrent force,' he said, 'can never be adequate.'

The programme was defeated in the Assembly by 264 to 213 but the Government had invoked the provisions of the Constitution of the Fifth Republic which required an absolute majority of all deputies against it to defeat the resolution. Technically, therefore, it carried. The Senate then rejected it, but it was passed in the same way three times by the Assembly and became law without the approval of the Senate. Thus, the fourth nuclear power is coming into existence against an overwhelming vote of the General Assembly of the United Nations and without a majority for the Government's plans in either of the houses of its own Parliament. One reason why the political hesitations were not expressed earlier is the fact that the Fourth Republic was particularly favourable to consistent policies pursued by a group of public servants with general support from a few politicians. This has been noted over railway modernisation, economic planning, relations with Europe and other issues—and the contrast between the changing mood of politicians and the consistent progress of the programme suggests that it was also true of nuclear weapons. Even in its early stages, an atomic weapons programme is highly technical and can be explained as a peaceful atomic programme or a mere option on weapons—at least until the questions of tests and a delivery system come up. Nevertheless, the French example, like the British, is likely to discourage as much as encourage those in other countries who give it close study.

The future is perhaps even more in doubt than in the case of Britain, which is spending somewhat more on its nuclear force, has tested its own thermo-nuclear weapons and (much more important) has obtained U.S. warhead designs and the opportunity to buy *Skybolt* and probably *Polaris*. France therefore has a long development road ahead both in warheads and in delivery systems. Although the subject is not yet mentioned, the possibility of a European force for the period after 1970 (when the plan is to replace the force based on the *Mirage 4*) must be getting serious consideration. Such a plan might be particularly acceptable to General de Gaulle's successors.

Chapter 5

Canada

CANADA is as special a case as France and the two can to some extent be looked at together. Both attained a general ability to build nuclear weapons early in the 1950s. Both pursued an expensive and ambitious programme of nuclear research while maintaining a generally loyal membership in the North Atlantic Treaty Organisation and relying on the United States Strategic Air Command for their security. As shown, France decided in 1955 to produce her own weapons and in 1960 to create a delivery system for them. Canada rejected this policy in 1946 by a deliberate and conscious decision at a time when she had considerable facilities on her soil and under her control. Alone among the nations up to the present, she has had the undoubted capacity to produce atomic bombs and has chosen not to do so. Her example is the direct refutation of a dangerous and inaccurate doctrine that no country able to produce nuclear weapons has resisted the temptation.[1] A horror of the weapons themselves has undoubtedly played a part in Canadian thinking; but so have a large number of special historical, military, geographical and political factors which condition the Canadian attitude to world affairs. These conditions do not exist anywhere else in quite the same way; but neither do the conditions which led the British and French Governments to the opposite conclusion. No two countries are in the same position.

Like Britain, Canada was involved in the Manhattan Project which produced the first atomic bombs during the Second World War. The laboratory established first at Montreal and later at Chalk River, near Ottawa, was the main base for

[1] e.g. 'So far no country has resisted the temptation to make its own atomic weapons once it has acquired the physical ability to do so.' Denis Healey, M.P., 'The Race against the H Bomb', *Fabian Tract* 322.

British experimental work on the wartime development of atomic energy. Canadian scientists played an important part in this and so did scientists from other parts of the Commonwealth. The Canadian Government decided to go on exploiting the assets embodied in Chalk River after the war and they commissioned their first nuclear reactor, known as NRX, as early as 1947. This reactor was designed to study the use of heavy water as a moderator. NRX itself could produce some tens of thousands of kilowatts of heat and Canadian scientists have devoted much of their energies since to developing this method of heat transfer. After a decade of development, it has become plain that reactors using heavy water have become one of the most promising lines for the industrial development of nuclear power. As this goes ahead, there is every prospect that Canada will play an increasingly prominent part. Even in countries with an advanced nuclear technology, such as Britain, Canadian experience is likely to be of value.

In fundamental research related to atomic energy, Canada is as well provided as any European country in proportion to her size. Chalk River employs several hundred scientists and several universities have had large government grants to build up their research in nuclear physics. Radio-active isotopes are widely used in scientific research and the techniques associated with them are widely understood. Looking at this position as a whole, it does not seem too much to say that Canada could have embarked on nuclear weapons with less effort than has been expended by France. She has within her own frontiers very large quantities of uranium ore and both the British and American weapons programmes have relied heavily on Canadian production, which has been bought from private producers under contracts by the Canadian Government. A public corporation, The Eldorado Mining and Refining Company, is the instrument of government policy in the marketing of uranium and produces several thousand tons of uranium oxide every year. With Britain and the United States, Canada has worked through the Combined Development Agency to obtain and market that part of the world's uranium which they could buy. When the agency started, it looked as if there would be strong competition for limited supplies of ore and the

Canadian Government agreed to the joint control of this market rather than allow a scramble for fortunes. In agreeing that the prices should be maintained at what the three nations regarded as reasonable levels, Canada probably realised that she was likely to lose financially; but the Canadian Government was anxious to avoid the disruption of booms and busts in the Canadian economy and wished to join the British and Americans in controlling the availability of uranium ore to smaller powers. Although the system seems to have been successful in its early years, the hope that it might go on has been frustrated by the discovery of uranium ores in many parts of the world.

The possession of large quantities of cheap hydroelectric power has given Canada an option to build uranium diffusion plants which she has not so far taken up. Serious consideration was given to the idea, but in 1951 it was turned down on economic grounds. It was thought then that the need for enriched uranium would not continue indefinitely and that the construction of a special dam for this purpose (as the Aluminium Company of Canada has done for its refineries at Arvida, Quebec and at Kitimat, British Columbia) would not be justified by a long enough productive life. Canadian atomic power thinking had already been directed away from enriched uranium by the choice of a heavy water cooling system.

As far as delivery systems are concerned, Canada would be well placed to compete in aircraft, though not in missiles. Because of her defence doctrine, which will be discussed later, she has made no effort to produce bombers; but she has shown her technical capacity by bringing the Avro *Arrow*, the CF–105, to the prototype stage. This long-range supersonic fighter would have reached full service by mid-1962 when it would probably have held the world's absolute speed record and would undoubtedly have been the most effective weapon in the air defence of North America.

The country also has the capacity to develop advanced aero-engines. Orenda Engines Limited developed the Orenda engine for the *Sabre* fighter (which gave it higher performance than its original American engine) and the very powerful Iroquois engine for the *Arrow*. It is true that Canadian technology in both aircraft and aero-engines depends heavily on

American and British experience—a relationship which is reflected in the ownership of the main Canadian companies by either American or British companies—but the fact remains that the capacity is in Canada and at the disposition of the Canadian Government.

Why then has Canada not embarked on a nuclear weapons programme? The most obvious reason is that as a nation it does not feel in danger now or for the future; but a consistently strong motive has been the fear of encouraging the spread of nuclear weapons and so complicating the problem of disarmament. The point that Canada knows herself to be a vital interest of the United States has been put by Professor James Eayrs of the University of Toronto:

> The construction of our own nuclear weapons system, costly and difficult as it would be, is not beyond our financial and technological capacity, as it is clearly beyond the capacity of any other presently non-nuclear NATO member excepting West Germany. But, altogether fortunately, our occupancy of the northern half of the North American continent makes such expense and effort wholly unnecessary. Any atomic attack upon North America would bring about United States retaliation. The Soviet Union, therefore, cannot under imaginable circumstances contemplate a nuclear strike directed specifically against Canada. The American apparatus for massive retaliation serves to deter attack on Canada precisely to the same extent that it serves to deter attack on the United States itself. We are the sole ally of the United States of which this can be said.[1]

There has been no fear of a declining credibility of the American commitment to Canada as there is to Western Europe. It is certainly possible to argue that if there is anything for Britain, France or West Germany to fear for the present or future of the American nuclear guarantee, Canada might well feel it as well: but Canadians feel too much, not too little, the presence of the United States. One distinguished Canadian soldier, Lieutenant General Guy Simonds (a former

[1] 'Canada, NATO, and Nuclear Weapons', *RCAF Staff College Journal*, 1960.

Chief of the General Staff), has said that 'Canada's defence needs could best be met by dividing her military effort between a retaliatory capability based on the atomic submarine and a properly balanced and organised tri-service striking force.'[1] But almost no one has taken up this view. Indeed, the Prime Minister, Mr. Diefenbaker, made the following categorical statement in the House of Commons on February 20th, 1959: "It is the policy of the Canadian Government not to undertake the production of nuclear weapons in Canada." The official military view was given by General Charles Foulkes, who was until 1960 Chairman of the Chiefs of Staff Committee and the most powerful figure in Canadian defence policy. It was, he said, 'inconceivable that Canada would wish to use nuclear weapons except . . . as an ally of the United States.' He felt that there was no case for the Canadian production of nuclear arms and argued that this would only encourage their spread to other powers.[2]

Unlike Britain and France, Canada therefore feels no need to insure against either American isolation or the possibility of a successful blackmail of the United States by a hostile power. Equally, she feels much less anxiety about her influence in Washington. Canadian governments have never feared that the issues of war and peace would be settled wrongly if they were not at the centre of negotiations. Both Britain and France feel deeply on this subject and have financed nuclear forces partly as a way of asserting parity of a kind with the Americans and Russians. With a population of 18 millions and modest armed forces (135,000 all-regular), Canada has no such pretensions. She regards herself as a middle power. In NATO, she keeps up the pressure against any small directorate of the British, French and Americans and in favour of general consultation; but she reluctantly accepts negotiations by the big three or big four (including West Germany) but would not tolerate the addition of any further countries (such as Italy) while she was excluded. The truth is that for many years

[1] *The Times* Supplement on Canada, London, November 24th, 1958.
[2] 'Canadian Defence in a Nuclear Age', Canadian Institute of International Affairs, May 1961.

Canada has prided herself as much on her influence in the United Nations as in Washington or NATO. In the early days of the U.N., Canada found herself in a strong position. On the basis of close relations with the United States, she acted as a highly successful bridge between many of the new nations (particularly India) and the American Government. More recently, the centre of the UN has shifted away from the West and Canada has played a less obvious part. Nevertheless, a major object of policy has been to create and maintain good relations with a large number of Afro-Asian countries. This very strong tendency in Canadian foreign policy was reflected in the attitude to the Anglo-French Suez ultimatum, in the accusation by M. Spaak at NATO in 1960 that there was an 'Oslo-Ottawa' axis, and the general notion that Canada, in spite of her NATO membership, was to be found among the 'white neutralists'. This is merely a tendency in Canadian policy; very strong loyalty to the western alliance is more fundamental. But on the narrow issue of influence, it is with the emerging nations of the world that Canada is trying to expand her points of contact, and not only with the United States. Thus insofar as nuclear weapons policy is determined by the desire to increase influence, this weighs in the Canadian case against building the bomb.

Purely military factors at first influenced Canada in the same way but have more recently become confused by the development of allied doctrine. In her non-nuclear mood, Canada adopted three main roles for her armed forces: balanced conventional army brigades for the defence of both Canadian soil and Western Europe; an advanced interceptor air force to serve in Canada and in Europe; and an anti-submarine navy to serve mainly in the North Atlantic as part of NATO's effort to sustain its sea communications. These were the sort of military jobs which the Canadian armed forces did in the Second World War. Although large numbers of Canadians had helped to man R.A.F. Bomber Command, strategic bombing had not been a primary part of the effort of the R.C.A.F. The decision to go over to an air force designed for air defence did not therefore alter an existing service structure. The contrast here with Britain is obvious. Once the strategic use of air power had been ruled out, the decision to abjure nuclear weapons was greatly simplified.

Canadian development effort was matched to these clear-cut roles. In addition to producing a class of advanced anti-submarine frigates and underwater weapons, the Canadian aircraft industry developed an effective maritime patrol aircraft and two interceptors. The first of these interceptors, the CF-100, was deployed both for home defence and with the air division which was put at the disposal of NATO in Europe. An advanced supersonic interceptor designed particularly for the air defence of North America, the CF-105 *Arrow*, was then undertaken as a major national effort. This was cancelled in 1959 at a time when western intelligence had come to the apparently inaccurate conclusion that the Russians were abandoning long-range bombers. The cost of the programme had steadily risen and showed every sign at that time that it would absorb an excessive share of the defence budget.

In this period, the Canadian Government had to face a very difficult series of decisions associated with the progress of tactical nuclear weapons in United States defence doctrine— and, by extension, in both NATO and North American Air Defence (NORAD) doctrine. In Europe it was decided that the eight squadrons of F-86 interceptors and four squadrons of CF-100 interceptors would be replaced by eight squadrons of Canadian-built Lockheed *Starfighters*, which the R.C.A.F. has designated the CF-104. What was much more important than this modernisation, however, was the decision under the 1957 NATO plan to switch the air defence squadrons in Europe over to a primary role of strike and reconnaissance. The strike part of this derived from the decision to give the allied forces on the Central Front a substantial dual capability, able to fire either nuclear or conventional weapons. Canada has thus taken on a heavy bombing role, even if it is with light aircraft. The nuclear weapons are to be American and kept under United States control; but this involves the R.C.A.F. in nuclear weapons in a way which conflicts with the Canadian Government's traditional policy and with its disarmament policy. This problem will arise later in 1962 when the CF-104s start into service and the change of roles takes effect. It has already arisen in the Canadian Brigade in Europe, where MC-70 provides for re-equipment with the American *Honest John* short-range unguided tactical missile. This, too, has a duel capability; and it has brought the dilemma to a head in Ottawa. In the air defence of Canada, the cancellation of the CF-105 and the replacement of it by two squadrons of the unmanned *Bomarc* and five squadrons of the American F-101B *Voodoo* interceptor have also produced problems. The *Bomarc* is designed for nuclear warheads and the *Voodoo* has the nuclear *Falcon* missile as an optional weapon. It seems likely that while the *Voodoos* will be operated with conventional missiles, an arrangement for U.S. weapons for the *Bomarc* is as unavoidable as one over the CF-104s and *Honest Johns*.

Military pressure for what the soldiers regard as essential modern weapons is being strongly applied. They are less concerned with who builds or controls them than their opposite numbers in Britain and France. As a result, the true basis for the Canadian non-nuclear policy of the last decade is now having to be thought out and expounded publicly. The Canadian Government has shown the extent to which it sees its position as a non-nuclear power as a source of prestige and is reluctant to part with it. There is also a strong element of morality—of conviction that the implication of possessing these weapons is that you might be prepared to use them in acts of mass destruction which are morally indefensible. There are other important influences. Hostility to nuclear armament is perhaps more firmly entrenched among politicians and officials in countries such as Canada, Norway, Sweden and Denmark than it is in Britain. The place of purely political conditions in the formation of military policy is stronger than in most countries because of a number of factors which weaken the influence of the Chiefs of Staff. For one thing Canada has always fought as a relatively small partner in larger wars directed by others and so it has never been possible to see the armed forces as the saviours of the country. For another, the forces have normally been maintained on a very modest basis in peacetime. The balance is thus weighed much more against conventional military views than in older countries.

The most severe arguments about nuclear weapons have

grown up since 1957, when the Norad agreement, uniting
Canadian and American air defences, was signed. This was in
fact just at the time when the Progressive Conservative Party
came into power after 22 years of Liberal administration. On
the showing of other countries, the Conservatives might have
been expected to take an easier line towards nuclear weapons
than the Liberals. In Canada however, this was complicated
by the traditional Conservative policy of national assertion
against the United States and by the fact that Mr. Diefenbaker
is personally profoundly influenced by the traditions of prairie
non-conformist radicalism. In general, the Liberals in opposition (led by Mr. Lester Pearson) have not allowed themselves
to drift to the right of the Conservatives. The result has been a
competition to avoid being the first to favour the adoption by
Canada of nuclear weapons while also avoiding charges of
feebleness towards the alliance. Because of the passions which
surrounded the cancellation of the *Arrow*, the *Bomarc* (which
was immediately named as its successor) has become a symbol
of the argument. It has become well known to the Canadian
public and the two bases which are being built in Ontario and
Quebec are opposed by those who dislike the Americans, those
who think defence against bombers is futile, those who dislike
nuclear weapons, those who resent the intrusion of the guided
weapon into the role of the fighter, and those who think the
Bomarc is another unsuccessful American weapon being sold to
gullible allies. The Liberal Party has naturally concentrated
much of its fire on such a handsome target. Nevertheless, it is
interesting that early in January 1961, the party made the more
general appeal to Canadians not to accept nuclear weapons
if offered them. It suggested that Canada should stay in
NATO, but withdraw from the programme for the *Bomarc* and
for interceptors while co-operating with the United States in
air detection and warning. Constant emphasis is put by the
Liberals on Canada's role in stopping the spread of weapons:
and Mr. Pearson has urged the government 'to reject the use
of any kind of nuclear weapons from its territory'.

Inside the Government, there has been a clear conflict.
Backed by military opinion and responding to NATO and
American pressure, the Department of Defence under Mr.

Douglas Harkness has made a strong case for the adoption of American nuclear warheads under dual control in all the categories where it seems to be desirable. Mr. Howard Green, the Minister of External Affairs, has fought this equally bitterly with support from some of his most senior and influential officials. Mr. Green is personally opposed to nuclear weapons and believes that Canadians should have nothing to do with them. He also argues that the work the country is doing in the United Nations and with the emergent countries would be made more difficult if Mr. Harkness had his way. The Prime Minister, Mr. Diefenbaker, has held his hand. If, as seems likely, the generals finally win, it is conceivable that a period in which the country becomes accustomed to the fact that it possesses nuclear weapons as an essential element in its defence may lead to a desire to acquire Canadian nuclear weapons under national control. Certainly the moral objections as such must lose some of their force if the troops are once equipped with them, even under dual control.

The impact of Canada as the first deliberately non-nuclear nation has been regrettably small; indeed, even the advocates of a non-nuclear club in Britain and elsewhere have seldom noticed that the club already has a member. Professor Eayrs asks whether Canada's abstention is likely to do anything towards keeping the number of independent centres of control over atomic weapons to the present four. 'Everything indicates it is not,' he says. 'The Afro-Asian nations have professed contempt for nuclear strategy not least because it has hitherto appeared beyond their grasp. But the atomic bomb is a potent international status symbol, luring even so mature a country as France into extravagant effort it can ill afford. Will it not exert an even stronger attraction on newly independent nations when the means to nuclear powerdom become available to them through cheaper and simpler methods of manufacture, to say nothing of an illicit atomic weapons trade? When Communist China explodes its first nuclear device, the Afro-Asian atomic arms race will be on'.[1] The debate may go on in Canada for many years in these terms.

In the group of countries which are on the verge of building

[1] *Op cit.*

nuclear weapons or have already built them, Canada seems an odd case. She does not think her presence in the highest counsels is indispensable to peace; she does not fear desertion by her allies; and she cherishes no tradition of military grandeur. But in citing France in the context of the newer nations, Professor Eayrs may prove to have been curiously wrong. He may find that the Afro-Asians develop much more along the lines of his own country than along French lines. Canadian moral feelings may not be very widely shared (though this is not yet clear), but Canada's position with modest armed forces, an anxiety to spend money primarily on economic development, and lack of ambition to be anything like a great power is likely to be repeated again and again.

Chapter 6

Germany

THE Federal Republic of Germany is an advanced nation, comparable industrially to the two most recent nuclear powers: Britain and France. In many specifically military technologies, it is true, a decade of restriction and neglect between 1945 and 1955 has left important gaps. But there can be no doubt that the very strong economy which developed at that time in a Germany free of the burden of military spending could easily fill these gaps and is already spreading into aircraft, guided weapons, rockets and other important areas. In three respects, however, Germany is in a very different position from her major European NATO partners:

1. She has undertaken by unilateral declaration (in the context of treaty arrangements with her European allies) not to manufacture nuclear weapons on her own soil;

2. A decision to embark on a national nuclear weapons industry in defiance of this undertaking would seriously and perhaps fundamentally alter her alliances;

3. The response of the Soviet Union to such a programme would undoubtedly be as violent as the state of the German-American alliance at that time allowed. No other country would face so dangerous a gestation period.

The precise wording of the 1955 renunciation was as follows:

The Federal Chancellor declares that the Federal Republic undertakes not to manufacture in its territory any atomic weapons, chemical or biological weapons.'[1]

Atomic weapons were defined as

'any weapon which contains, or is designated to contain,

[1] Annex I to Protocol No. III on the Control of Armaments under the Brussels Treaty of March 17th, 1948, *Bundesgesetzblatt*, 1955, Nr. 7, Bonn March 25th, 1955.

or utilise, nuclear fuel or radioactive isotopes and which, by explosion or other uncontrolled nuclear transformation of the nuclear fuel, or by radio-activity of the nuclear fuel or radioactive isotopes, is capable of mass destruction, mass injury or mass poisoning. Furthermore, any art, device, assembly or material especially designed for, or primarily useful in, any weapon [as defined] shall be deemed to be an atomic weapon.'[1]

The parties to Western European Union (Britain, France, Germany, Italy, Luxembourg, Belgium and the Netherlands) then agreed as follows: 'The High Contracting Parties, members of Western European Union, take note of and record their agreement with the Declaration of the Chancellor of the Federal Republic of Germany (made in London on October 3rd, 1954 and annexed hereto as Annex I) in which the Federal Republic of Germany undertook not to manufacture in its territory atomic, biological and chemical weapons. The types of armaments referred to in this Article are defined in Annex II. These armaments shall be more closely defined and the definitions brought up to date by the Council of the Western European Union.'[2]

It will be noted that this statement contains no renunciation of the possession or use of nuclear weapons, nor of their production on the territory of other countries. Germany has not renounced a nuclear strategy; she has merely renounced an independent nuclear weapons industry. There is no significant group in Germany which openly expresses the conviction that the 1954 declaration should be reversed and there is no reason to believe that it is widely held. But this should not be taken to mean that Germany has renounced nuclear weapons. The official view, indeed, is that the country's defence cannot be anything but nuclear. The Federal Government is convinced that German soil has been defended by nuclear weapons for more than a decade and it is determined that this defence shall remain. It believes, however, that there is much in the view that the British and French nuclear deterrents are com-

[1] *Ibid.*, Annex II, Paragraph I.
[2] Protocol No. III, Part I, Article 1.

paratively ineffective and that the only reliable answer to the
Soviet Union is a force of the size and variety of that of the
United States. As a result German policy is primarily concerned to commit the United States as completely as possible to
an overwhelming response to any aggression on the East-West
frontier and to reinforce any weaknesses in American credibility
with NATO, European or Franco-German arrangements.

Discontent with the present allied arrangements can be
traced to the two quite separate issues of prestige (or equality)
and defence. At present, prestige is playing a small part in
government thinking, though it would probably make much
more appeal to public opinion than the military considerations which carry such weight in Bonn. But it can be seen at
present in the insistence that there must be no discrimination
as between one NATO partner and another. For some years
this has been a major theme in all public statements. The
Federal Government has made it clear that it will accept no
new limitations on its sovereignty which are not accepted by
other members of the alliance. Germany's allies have been put
on notice that nothing which could be regarded as an extension of the discriminatory spirit of the London Agreements can
be contemplated. In particular, the Federal Government has
insisted that the alliance should refuse to consider any plans
for thinning out forces in Central Europe, for open skies over
Germany (when this does not involve the Soviet Union), for the
withdrawal of nuclear weapons from forward areas (including,
obviously, most or all of the Federal Republic) or any other
such commitment. The persistent interest of the British Government in such plans between 1955 and 1960 seriously damaged
relations between the two countries.

The Federal Government has equally refused to coun-
tenance any extension of its non-nuclear commitment to a
treaty involving the Soviet Union because it says that this
would give its potential enemy an unacceptable say in its long-
term defence policy. The restrictions on sovereignty now
in effect were not made to the concert of powers or to the
international community as a whole: they were given to
Western European Union and are, so to speak, the private
affair of Western Europe. The issue of equality for Germany in

this sense is obviously one of the profound issues of policy which divides the Russians from the Americans and their allies. The Soviet Union may be expected to use all its diplomatic resources to keep the issue alive as long as it has any hope of results.

Within the NATO alliance itself, the issue of equality has recurred constantly in official German references to the arming of NATO troops in Europe. This and the German conviction that the defence of Europe must be nuclear were most clearly stated by the Inspector General of the Bundeswehr in an appendix to the forces bulletin in 1961. He wrote:

> In the event of a unilateral renunciation of atomic weapons for the shield forces the Federal Republic cannot be defended. The presence of these weapons prevents the opponent from massing and concentrating his forces, without hesitation, for swift strikes. If one's own troops had to fight without tactical atomic weapons, there would be a much greater possibility that the opponent might overrun the European defences. . . . The renunciation of tactical atomic weapons enforces either the use of strategic atomic weapons or surrender.
>
> The Bundeswehr must have the same effective armaments as the allied shield forces. The shield force of NATO must be a whole. Otherwise the opponent would choose for the centre of his attack the units with inferior arms. The soldiers of the Bundeswehr have a right to weapons which are at least equal to those of the opponent. Responsibility for the soldiers entrusted to them compels the military leaders to request atomic arms, which in the present situation are indispensable for the shield force. Otherwise there is a danger that the soldiers will be confronted with impossible tasks and their self-confidence will be undermined. . . .
>
> In order to deter any attempt to employ military force against the Federal Republic, the Bundeswehr is obliged to be armed for any possible form of military conflict. An army whose technical inferiority is clear in advance represents no deterrent risk for the opponent. Its effectiveness is not credible. A defender with bow and arrow has never deterred

an attacker with firearms. Those who want effective national defence cannot close their eyes to the necessity of arming the shield force with atomic weapons.'[1]

This theme has been repeatedly expressed by the Federal Government. Two statements among many by Herr Strauss, the Minister of Defence, may be quoted:

The renunciation of nuclear weapons for the Central European shield forces would mean no less than the weakening of the European periphery of our alliance by more than 90 per cent of its firepower. This could not even be balanced by corresponding reductions in a limited European area on the other side of the Iron Curtain, since, contrary to the West, the U.S.S.R. would always retain the possibility of refilling this so-called atom-free zone with nuclear weapons at any time.[2]

That very justifiable expression, the 'distribution of tasks within NATO', should surely not be taken to mean that whilst there is a tactical atomic weapon deterrent in the sectors occupied by Anglo-Saxon or other non-German forces, there is none in those sectors occupied by the Germans. The idea of incorporating American or British atomic weapon units in German divisions merely in order to satisfy the principle of not placing such weapons in German hands has been absolutely and completely rejected by the allies.[3]

The military doctrine is clear and unequivocal: the defence of Germany must be nuclear and the weapons must be in the hands of the troops so that there can be no doubt that they will be used. Serious doubts about whether the United States Government still accepts this doctrine have arisen since the Kennedy Administration came into office. Herr Strauss was particularly concerned at the publication of Henry Kissinger's *The Necessity of Choice* in which he argued in favour of conventional rather than nuclear responses in order to impose

[1] *Survival*, November-December, 1960, p. 253.
[2] Interview September 29th, 1961, with the *Politisch-Soziale Korrespondenz*, official translation.
[3] 'The Clear Conception', speech by Herr Strauss, 1961, official translation.

a pause. Talk about raising the nuclear threshold has aroused profound suspicions about the likely response of the United States President to an incursion into Germany. Hamburg is virtually on the zonal frontier, Berlin is 100 miles inside enemy territory and even Frankfurt is only 120 miles from Thuringia: to what adventures might the Russians be tempted if they knew there was a gap before nuclear weapons would be used and that NATO policy was to bring the action to a halt by imposing a pause? This question is being very seriously asked in Bonn and Herr Strauss and the Government appear to be profoundly disturbed about the existing position. Essentially it is a crisis of credibility. In the German Government's view 'those countries which do not belong to the "nuclear club" are practically defenceless as long as the deterrent effect of nuclear weapons is not at their disposal.'[1] While Mr. Dulles was at President Eisenhower's side and the Russian long-range air and missile forces were not effective against North America, it believed that the deterrent effect of American strategic nuclear weapons was at the disposal of the Federal Republic. In the conditions of 1962, it does not. A preference for conventional strategies is observable in Washington and the direct threat to America goes on growing. The German Government has thus become convinced that arrangements must be found which will give them a reliable nuclear defence. Herr Strauss has said that 'a coalition' with a great power is no longer enough;[2] yet isolation from the United States is unthinkable. 'What we have to do in NATO,' Herr Strauss has said, is to find some formula ensuring on the one hand that no focal points of crisis arise in which the United States would be constantly facing the greatest risk to mankind that has ever been known, whilst on the other giving the remaining parties to the alliance the certainty that the major party to the alliance is ready to take that ultimate risk if it is a matter of protecting other NATO partners from a genuine attack by an aggressor.'[3]

[1] Frank C. Nash Memorial Lecture at Georgetown University given by Herr Strauss, November 17th, 1961, official translation.

[2] 'Common Security-Common Policy—The decisive questions for the future of the Atlantic Alliance'—by Herr Strauss, official translation.

[3] *Ibid.*

In seeking this formula, a whole series of possibilities have been explored. Herr Strauss appealed in a speech at Georgetown University in November, 1961, for an Atlantic Union; he has asked[1] for a 'formula which gives all the members of the community a common guarantee that all will enjoy the same measure of security'; the possibility of a European deterrent has been mentioned from time to time; and there is some co-operation between French and German scientists which could conceivably be developed into a significant military arrangement. If a form of Atlantic Union or European Union were to come which embraced full political and military integration, Germany would be one of the first to grasp it. The NATO deterrent idea is designed to give a comparable commitment with nuclear weapons in the absence of political union or confederation. One of the most straightforward expositions of the German attitude was contained in Herr Strauss's proposal that the Supreme Allied Commander, Europe, should be empowered to use the alliance's nuclear weapons in the defence of any member's territory at the request of that government. Under this system, Germany would have no nuclear weapons, but she would have an unambiguous nuclear defence. This was rejected in Washington, if not in Paris. The United States, while offering encouragement to the NATO deterrent idea if a suitable formula could be found, has gone no farther than the offer of five *Polaris* submarines under the almost entirely national arrangements which cover the NATO commitment of the Sixth Fleet in the Mediterranean.[2] A number of complex formulas about control by members of the NATO Standing Group have been put forward and even a voting procedure which gave the United States a veto provided she had one or two small nations on her side. It is possible that a compromise might be reached; but it is becoming increasingly obvious that the Kennedy Administration at least—which

---

[1] In a lecture on German policy broadcast by the Hessian Broadcasting Company, December 6th, 1960.

[2] In a speech at Ottawa on May 17th, 1961, President Kennedy added 'Beyond this, we look to the possibility of eventually establishing a NATO sea-borne missile force, which would be truly multilateral in ownership and control'.

will remain in office until January, 1965—is not prepared to give away effective control of the decisions over war and peace and over the even more difficult decisions about the precise response to particular situations. It may be prepared to go further in consultation and joint planning—*contrôle*, in the French sense—but Washington seems as determined to keep the final say as Bonn is to bring it across the Atlantic. The Germans may not be an irresistible force (if only because they fully recognise their dependence on the United States) and Mr. Kennedy may prove to be a moveable object: but serious students of the subject in both capitals have concluded that no formula is possible which can meet the requirements of both sides.

If this proves to be true by the end of 1962 (the date Herr Strauss has set), what will Germany do? It seems clear that she will explore every possibility of unified European defence which does not involve any withdrawal of the present United States commitment. British willingness to enter into a European nuclear force as a preliminary to a confederation of some kind might attract American patronage and would certainly be attractive to Germany. If, as seems likely, British public opinion is not prepared to move into Europe at this speed, an arrangement might still be reached with France. A certain amount of basic scientific co-operation may already be taking place on some military issues related to atomic weapons between the two countries. The determination of the French Government to get a nuclear defence of Europe into European hands and the concern about the cost of an effective national *force de frappe* would make co-operation with Germany a logical step. No formal breach of the terms of the renunciation of 1955 would be involved in a system under which France manufactured nuclear weapons and Germany concentrated on delivery systems. There is evidence that both countries favour the use of sea-based rocket weapons because of the limited area of Western Europe—a solution which has found favour in even such large areas as the United States and Russia. A Franco-German bilateral arrangement for the provision of nuclear weapons would have a perfectly respectable parallel in NATO in the arrangements which the United States has reached bilaterally with a number of countries.

There is as yet no reason to believe that the French Government will show the inhibitions about sharing which the American and British Governments have shown.

If all these possibilities failed, would the Federal Republic embark on its own weapons programme? And may it already have done so in secret? The official line, in spite of the strong statements of the need for a nuclear defence, is that it would not and has not. The opposition Social Democratic Party has strongly criticised the Government's pro-nuclear policy, as a source of fear in the alliance and propaganda for the Russians; and it has also accused Herr Strauss of encouraging the spread of nuclear weapons. It regards this as a major evil and would be strongly committed, both emotionally and historically, against it if returned to office. The Government has replied, as it has done on all defence questions for some years, that what it is doing is at the insistence of its NATO allies and to meet the plans of the NATO high command. Bonn's influence in the alliance has grown to the point where the suggestion that it does not think or plan for itself can only be regarded as spurious. Nevertheless, the Government has repeatedly said that it has no desire to obtain a national nuclear weapons production facility and has denounced the spread of weapons. In appealing for a NATO deterrent, Herr Strauss asked for 'a practicable political and technical formula conducive to preventing any spread of the production of nuclear weapons.'[1] He has said: 'The Government of the Federal Republic of Germany has never been in favour of the group of nations possessing atomic weapons being expanded. They have always been against it. In this instance, they have given particularly strong support to the American point of view that the production of atomic weapons should not be extended beyond the present group of producers.'[2] Only in the event of a failure to get an effective arrangement with NATO, with Western Europe, or with France is a national solution likely to be considered. This would so increase the country's vulnerability and would be so costly that it is unlikely to be done without American support, however reluctant.

[1] In the Hessian Broadcast, above.
[2] In 'The Clear Conception' above.

The position which can broadly be assumed to be that of the Social Democratic Party (though they are by no means committed to it) is that put forward by Herr Helmut Schmidt:

It is in Germany's interest to limit the further spread of nuclear weapons. The Federal Republic would be well advised to follow the example of Sweden in its statements on nuclear weapons. During the winter of 1959–60 the Swedish Government postponed for five years the decision to go over to nuclear weapons so as to give support during this period to the general efforts to close the Nuclear Club. The Swedish Government will only make a final decision if, by the end of the period, there is no prospect of closing the doors of the Nuclear Club and halting the further spread of nuclear weapons. The intention is that, in the meantime, it should continuously observe and examine the premises, consequences, advantages and disadvantages of such a decision. Such a policy would be to the advantage of the Federal Republic also. It would not by any means prevent the Federal Republic from making an authoritative and professional contribution to NATO's consultations and decisions on matters of nuclear organisation and strategy ... The danger of the Soviet Union's being provoked to preventive aggression will grow from that moment on when the Federal Republic appears able, if need be, to conduct an independent and autonomous foreign policy backed by the power of nuclear weapons.[1]

Technically, however, it should be recorded that there is a substantial amount of uranium ore in the Federal Republic, mainly in the south-east. There would probably be enough to support a programme for making up to a dozen bombs a year. The federal structure of the country held up the development of atomic energy in the first decade after the Second World War and the Federal Government would probably have difficulty in publicly financing a weapons programme. Nevertheless, atomic development since 1955 has been rapid and well-directed. Ancillary industries have been established in a

[1] *Defence or Retaliation*, translated by Edward Thomas, Oliver and Boyd, 1962, 173–4.

number of fields such as the manufacture of graphite. Research reactors have been built at four places, though these are supplied with fuel from outside the country under the normal safeguards. A modest power programme has been started, and will no doubt accelerate in the sixties. The acquisition of a delivery system would be expensive but probably not impossible to solve, even for a modern invulnerable system. Like France, Germany is interested in vertical take-off aircraft; and the Rolls-Royce RB-162 vertical lift engine, which is probably the most advanced in the world, is being developed jointly by the German firm of M.A.N. under an Anglo-German agreement. More vulnerable, but effective American systems are already going into service in the German forces in large numbers. The most important of these is the F.104 *Starfighter* supersonic fighter-bomber which is being produced inside the country. A testing ground for a strictly national nuclear weapon might be difficult to find.

A clandestine nuclear weapons programme at this stage seems most unlikely. Reactors or diffusion plants are virtually impossible to hide and there are plenty of people watching for them. The country is still covered with foreign troops, is an open society, and its plants are subject to inspection by the W.E.U. Arms Control Agency. The Federal Government was surprised to discover what suspicions of its intentions remained among its allies over the private negotiations which it began in 1960 with the Spanish Government for ordinary bases and training facilities. If it was working now towards a clandestine bomb, it could innocently expand its nuclear power programme: but it has been in no hurry to do this. A discouraging line has been taken about the economics of nuclear power and progress towards stations which would produce plutonium in significant weapons quantities has been slower than it might have been with military encouragement.

Nevertheless, there is an air of suspended judgment on these questions in West Germany. The country cannot see any way to step beyond its American guarantee and everything depends, at present, on how far that can be stretched. No non-nuclear power says with more determination that it must have nuclear weapons for its defence; yet none (except possibly

Israel) must make a more perilous leap to get them. That is why Germany stands uncertainly looking at the brink; some of those who lead the country undoubtedly want a federal solution for the Atlantic Alliance; others hope that Europe will become a third great power. Although Germany is probably the non-nuclear country most able technically and industrially to follow the French, its political reasons for holding back are at present decisive.

Chapter 7
China

NAPOLEON'S plea that China should be left to sleep is certainly echoed in the West and may also be in the hearts of the Russians. No power wants to see another major actor coming on the scene. But what they want and what they expect are two very different things. Everywhere, it is being assumed that China is forging ahead rapidly with industrialisation and with modern weapons. In Washington, serious opinions are expressed that the Chinese Government is about to explode its first bomb; and any assiduous reader of the press, particularly the Indian press, will find that Chinese nuclear explosions were reported in Sinkiang in 1955 and in Lanchow in 1959; and regular reports that China is on the verge of a test appear from a variety of sources.

Quite obviously China is not sleeping and her 600,000,000 vigorous people must be taken seriously. Behind the wall of security, little is known of what is going on. Even in so basic a thing as food production, the world knows only of the revolutionary commune programme of 1957–8, the ambitious claims for agricultural production in 1959, and the calamitous year in 1960 in which starvation seems to have become a serious threat. One thing we do know is that, of all countries, China is least able to trade with the West in materials which might have strategic significance. Extensive agreements seem to have been made with the Russians in the mid-1950s, but by 1960 relations were bad and technicians were being withdrawn in large numbers. Such things as the nuclear reactor near Peking and the production line for MiG-17s reflect a period of useful and productive co-operation between Russia and China. What has happened since is much less clear. If there was a programme for nuclear weapons, it seems reasonable to expect Russian withdrawal to have accompanied the withdrawal of the technicians in 1960.

Since it is not possible to go to Peking and talk with the men who are taking the decisions—as it is possible to go to Bonn, Ottawa, New Delhi or Stockholm—nothing can be said reliably about the decisions which have been taken or are likely to be taken. All that one can do is to examine the few pieces of published evidence and then lay out the technical factors which together with the military and political facts of China's position must bear on the decision. On the whole these produce a more cautious estimate of Chinese capacity than the general American view. In the absence of Russian help, the cost of becoming a nuclear power will be very high to China. The earlier it is seriously tried, the more, relatively, it will cost. As the industrial and scientific base widens, the job becomes easier; if it is attempted at high priority early in the 1960s (remembering that China's published objective is to reach the industrial strength of Britain by 1970) it will hamper other sectors. The issue then becomes one of military urgency. Presumably the time-scale which has been adopted was determined by the views of the high command about the advantages to China of an early stock of weapons with a primitive delivery system. Both in real military terms and on the issue of prestige, there is room for two quite opposite points of view. If this chapter tends to emphasize the objections, it is partly because they have received so little attention and partly because they became as obvious in the case of China as in that of other underdeveloped countries. The case for going slowly into nuclear weapons is as strong for Communist China as it is for India; but that does not mean that, at the highest levels of the party and government, it has won out.

The most immediate difficulty in assessing the future of nuclear power in China is that of knowing what technical facilities exist and of how these will be deployed in the next few years. A part of the reason for this is the substantial isolation of China from the rest of the world in scientific and technical affairs. Chinese scientists are much rarer visitors to the West than Russians have ever been, while the extent to which Chinese scientific literature is read in the West is virtually negligible. Thus it is inevitable that estimates about the capacity or the intention of the Chinese to carry through some technical project must be attended by the most serious uncertainties.

Published information about Chinese accomplishments in the exploitation of atomic energy refers only to a single reactor built near Peking as part of an agreement for technical assistance by the Soviet Union, and commissioned in the middle of 1958. The reactor is fuelled with enriched uranium, and cooled by ordinary ('light') water. Its thermal power is nominally 5000 kW., and in this respect and others it resembles the reactors known as PLUTO and DIDO which have been in operation at Harwell, in the United Kingdom, for several years. Most probably the Peking reactor can be operated at a power somewhat greater than that for which it was designed, and if the device were to be used exclusively for the production of military plutonium, it could be expected to yield up to 2.5 kilograms a year.

The assumption that the Peking reactor has been used exclusively for the production of military plutonium has in the past been used as a means of estimating the date at which the first Chinese nuclear device would be exploded. If it is calculated that five kilograms of plutonium could be obtained by the operation of the reactor at full power for just over two years from the autumn of 1958, the Chinese would have enough irradiated fuel rods containing plutonium for one bomb by the end of 1960. Six months later this could have been extracted in a rudimentary chemical separation plant and the explosion of a device could have taken place at any time after the summer of 1961. It is not ungenerous to suppose that this line of reasoning has been responsible for many of the suggestions that the first Chinese atomic explosion would be carried out in the second half of 1961.

Valuable though it may be as a means of illustrating what can be achieved with small resources, this argument is not a reliable guide to the realities of the Chinese approach to nuclear power. In the first place, there is no reason to think that the Chinese are actually allowed to retain for their own use the irradiated fuel supplied to them by the Soviet Union to keep the Peking reactor going. In its agreements for the fuelling of reactors in Egypt the Soviet Union has arranged that irradiated material should be returned to Russia, and there is every reason to expect that a similar arrangement would be in effect with China. Indeed what evidence there is suggests that in its dealings with China on nuclear questions the Soviet Union has avoided helping the Chinese towards military nuclear power. It is reasonable to assume that the Peking reactor is not contributing to the creation of a stock of military plutonium in China, but that it is being used for the purposes for which it was intended—the collection of scientific information and the training of scientists.

There is a still more compelling argument for believing that the Chinese would not wish to depend on the Peking reactor for supplies of military plutonium. For even if they were allowed to retain irradiated fuel, fresh fuel for the reactor can only be had from the Soviet Union, where the uranium enrichment plants are established. Thus it is most probable that a Chinese decision to manufacture atomic weapons would be followed immediately by the design and construction of a reactor using natural uranium as fuel, though not necessarily linked to the production of electricity, or even aimed at the design of civil atomic power stations. This, after all, has been the first step in each of the three Western programmes of military atomic power.

The difficulty here is, of course, that of knowing when the design of such a plant would have been started, how soon construction would have been completed and how quickly the fuel irradiated in the plant would have begun to yield military plutonium. The actual design of a plutonium producing reactor could no doubt have been attempted in China at any time in the last decade—certainly enough Chinese scientists with the necessary skill have been visitors at the Russian nuclear research centre at Dubna. The difficulties would have been mainly in the refining of uranium metal from indigenous ores; the assembly of the complex systems of instruments needed to supervise the operation of the plant; the commitment of something like a hundred creative scientists and engineers to the project; and the gathering of confidence that the design of the first plant could be accurate even in such matters as the acceptability of the impurities necessarily present in constructional materials.

Most probably the point at which China would have been physically and psychologically able to make such a commitment of its resources is to be placed around 1957 or 1958. Certainly it is known that during that period Chinese scientists were making significant contributions to such specialised crafts—entirely concerned with nuclear measurements—as the design of the instruments known as 'pulse-height analysers'—or 'kick-sorters'. During this period, too, the traffic of Chinese nationals to the research centre at Dubna became more conspicuous if not greater in volume.

On this assumption it is reasonable to suppose that in the development of military atomic power China must in 1958 have been further behind than was France in 1954—the date when the G-1 reactor was laid down. Moreover it is inconceivable that the Chinese could substantially have shortened the process of development undertaken in France, so that it is wise to suppose that the first Chinese atomic device cannot be exploded earlier than a date four years after the first French explosion (at the beginning of 1960). In other words, the first Chinese explosion is unlikely to be carried out before 1964, though 1963 is a possibility if a decision to commit resources was actually taken at the beginning of 1957. If—as may be the case—a Chinese decision to become a nuclear power was made later than 1958, the first explosion cannot be expected before a correspondingly later date than 1964.

But one bomb does not make a power great and if—as is most likely—a Chinese decision to manufacture nuclear weapons will in fact be a decision to become a substantial manufacturer, real proof of Chinese strength cannot come until much later. Even a vigorous programme of development cannot yield overnight the reactor designs and the finished plants needed to produce plutonium in bulk. In the British nuclear weapons programme, thirteen years were spent in producing ten plutonium producing reactors. Even if China is to content itself with such a comparatively modest nuclear strength as that which has been created in Britain, it is most improbable that this could be achieved before 1970. For this reason it is safe and indeed necessary to suppose that whenever the first Chinese nuclear explosion takes place, that country will not be able to manufacture nuclear weapons at a rate of some dozens a year until the end of the 1960s.

The prospects for an effective Chinese delivery system without Russian assistance do not seem to be good until at least 1975 and possibly (depending on technical advances) much later than that. What the Chinese have now is entirely owed to the Russians. Their largest capacity bomber is the Tu-4, the Russian equivalent of the B-29 which carried the first American atomic bombs. This would take a 10,000 pound-bomb over a radius of about 1,500 miles; but its vulnerability to all modern air defences is so great as to make it useless for anything but a superbly managed surprise attack. A more serious force is the large fleet of the Russian Il-28 twin-jet bombers—some estimates say there are as many as 700 of these. With the MiG-15 and MiG-17 fighters, which are assembled in Chinese plants, China can be said to have had a modern and effective air defence for the period between 1950 and 1960. From their own resources in that period, they built a trainer and a small transport aircraft.

The full modernisation of the Chinese Air Force with a new generation of Russian aircraft should now be underway. It is generally believed that the MiG-19 and MiG-21 fighters are on the way if they have not already been supplied; but the remarkable sight of four *Badger* bombers being sold to Indonesia while none have yet appeared in China demands explanation. These would be effective carriers of nuclear weapons and would be the first in any routine modernisation programme which could do the job with real reliability. Indeed, the Russians designed the *Badger* to carry nuclear bombs and for use against ships. If the Chinese are planning a small stockpile of bombs for the period after 1965, their first objective would obviously be to get some of these bombers—or, better still, the longer range *Bear* or one of the three new supersonic bombers. The issue may well be a difficult one between the two countries and could be producing the dilemma which Washington has felt about British and French nuclear weapons. If the Chinese Government is developing nuclear weapons, the Russians could decide to offer one of a number of options. They could offer conventional aircraft, such as the

Badger, which can also carry nuclear bombs; or they could offer co-operation on components and in the training of technicians; or they could decide to go in more deeply in the hope of closer political relations and ultimately of a return of information and assistance from the growing Chinese economy. For the moment, all these courses seem to have been rejected. It is at least probable that China is on her own. What should she do?

The first and most obvious option is a blackmail bomb with a primitive delivery system. It might well be argued that a simple test would have an immediate and decisive effect not only in Washington but in New Delhi, Tokyo, Formosa and, of course, Moscow. There is certainly evidence that the same people who scorn the French devices will be awed by the same thing from the Chinese—in spite of the fact that the Chinese have never produced a *Mirage 3* or a *Caravelle.* This tendency is already noticeable among the Americans. The old Hegelian notion of nations rising and falling dies hard and it has been allied with a fascination with the sheer numbers of China (though not, curiously, of India, where the problems of becoming a serious nuclear power are recognised). Whether this is reasonable or unreasonable, there can be no doubt that an explosion in a Chinese desert would produce far more effect than one in India or the Sahara. China's reputation for ruthlessness and military ambition is part of this. Just as nuclear weapons are valueless to a country with a reputation for moderation—such, for example, as Britain or Sweden—in political bargaining, they are of wholly disproportionate value to those who are thought to be ready to use them. It is true that in general Mr. Khrushchev (the only person who has so far tried it) has obtained few benefits from rattling rockets; but Russia's scrupulous avoidance of conflict outside the Communist block since 1945 may have contributed to a reputation for sanity which belies the noisy speeches. China has no such reputation. She has given the impression (somewhat falsely) of continuous fighting around her borders—in Korea, the offshore islands, Indo-china and Tibet—since the Communists came to power; and the two Chinas vow each other's extinction as regularly as the two Germanies or the two Koreas.

In this climate of opinion, China might well expect the possession of a bomb to strike fear into the small countries of south-east Asia. Those who feel that they must in the long run accept the primacy of China in the area might consider this a decisive fact. What would be the effect in Formosa, Japan and India? If it is felt in Peking that the hopes of the Kuomintang would be finally ended by a Communist Chinese bomb, it is possible that military opinion would be backing a high priority for the bomb to obtain the economy of a smaller and more modern army. But the excellence of the Formosan air defences have already been demonstrated and the Americans will obviously be prepared to improve them in the face of a nuclear threat. As long as the Chinese do not have a missile or much more advanced bomber to carry their nuclear weapons, their chances of penetrating to Formosa would be slim. There is also the possibility of American atomic weapons in Formosa under a dual veto arrangement. Nevertheless, the psychological advantages against Chiang Kai-shek would be great and probably constitute the strongest single argument for a high priority for nuclear weapons.

The effects on others might not be so encouraging. Japan's reaction would probably in the long run be the most important. Japan could build more nuclear weapons faster than China and she could create a more advanced delivery system. The deep aversion to atomic bombs in Japanese public opinion could conceivably be transformed into an urgent demand for a deterrent to renewed atomic attack on the Japanese islands if China began to emerge as a nuclear power. On the other hand, students of Japanese affairs find a widespread feeling of friendship towards China combined with hostility towards Russia. The Russian bomb has merely served to maintain the Japanese-American alliance; it has not stirred up demands for a similar programme in Japan. A Chinese bomb would undoubtedly have a more immediate impact on Japanese public opinion and on military thought. Peking's assessment of what this would be must be one of the most important factors in her present plans.

India's reaction would probably be a combination of the Japanese and that of the south-east Asian countries. No doubt

the immediate result would be a surge of national feeling—
such as was shown over the border disputes with the Chinese—
and a justifiable pride in the nuclear technology which India
has already achieved. A demand for nuclear weapons could be
satisfied within about a year any time after 1963 and there can
be little doubt that India too could produce more nuclear
weapons faster than China. As far as the Soviet Government is
concerned, the Tass communique of September 10th, 1959,
dissociating the Soviet Union from the Tibet operation should
not be forgotten. The offer of the MiG-19 fighter for the
Indian air force and the possibility of a Russian power reactor
for the Indian atomic energy programme cannot have been
welcome to those in China who anticipate that ultimately
they must come into conflict with India.

The most important unknown of the equation must be the
effect a Chinese bomb would have on Peking-Moscow relations. No doubt the Russians have said to the Chinese (as the
Americans said to the British and French) that national
atomic aspirations could only damage their alliance. There is a
considerable body of evidence that the Russians have been
doing what they could to persuade the Chinese to abjure
nuclear weapons. Nevertheless, the issue is not what the
Russians are saying but what the Chinese believe the Russians
will do once they have the bomb. They will certainly be
anxious to know whether Russia will sell or give advanced
delivery systems for it. This debate seems to have first been
conducted in 1955 in Peking and to have reached the conclusion that the Russians will not be moved to atomic co-
operation by a successful Chinese bomb programme. Since
then much thought must have been given to the matter and it
is very difficult to estimate the conclusion which the Government might have reached. Generally speaking, however,
sophisticated powers may be expected to show a certain lack of
interest in nuclear weapons which are not part of a modern
delivery system. Thus, China could expect a good nuclear
weapons force—the kind of thing they might hope to produce
in the 1975 to 1980 period—to have an impact on the Russians; anything less is likely to be confined in its impact to the
diminishing number of the unsophisticated.

What of the effect of a Chinese bomb on her military position? Once more, it becomes necessary to look at the wide variety of frontiers—the Nationalists to the east, the Russians to the north, the Indians to the southwest and the soft small states of south-east Asia to the south. On the east, the Chinese confront the Americans. The US Seventh Fleet creates an impenetrable barrier to Formosa, which the Chinese Government would like to capture by any possible means. One part of the answer to this fleet, a force of submarines, has already been supplied by the Russians with the provision of between 20 and 30 W class boats. In a determined attack, these could certainly do substantial damage. Would a small nuclear weapons force provide a valuable addition to them? The answer must be in the negative, since an attack on the Seventh Fleet with nuclear weapons must surely bring nuclear retaliation against the mainland of China. This would be the classic case of the small nuclear power creating the military situation in which it brought the greatest possible disaster on its country without effectively deterring anything. The Seventh Fleet's air defences are so good that none of the present Chinese aircraft would have a very good chance of penetration. It would be necessary to have a bomber with good supersonic performance or high speed low level performance.

With regard to Formosa itself, the military situation is more ambiguous. Obviously, Generalissimo Chiang Kai-shek could not be expected to produce a bomb from the resources of the island. But would the United States withhold some form of nuclear cooperation if there was a direct nuclear threat to Formosa from China? It may be doubted. Once again, China might face a superior nuclear power with more weapons carried by more advanced vehicles. Would Russia permit this? Can tacit American-Russian agreements to hold back the spread of weapons to allies be expected in these areas? If so, would these survive a successful national nuclear weapons programme on one side? Peking must decide.

Looking south, the Chinese Government can be expected to proceed by the methods of infiltration and subversion which have served it so well in the past. Although it fought a war in Korea which was in many ways sophisticated, it is through the

use of well trained infantry that the Chinese Communists have
arrived where they are. They may be expected to continue
this policy to the south, at least as long as they are unable to
match the numbers and sophistication of American nuclear
weapons. To fight with atomic bombs in the next decade, at
least, would be to fight on a battlefield of the enemy's choice.
The use of nuclear weapons against India would be as likely to
produce a nuclear response as their use against a member of
the South-East Asia Treaty Organisation. Apart from what
the Indians themselves might do if threatened by Chinese
bombs, it is obvious that the British, Americans and possibly
even the Russians would lend support to a non-nuclear India
under attack in this way. Certainly in the present climate of
world affairs the Chinese Government would be bold if it
believed that it could launch an attack on India with the
assurance that the Russian strategic deterrent lay behind it.
Since in conventional force the Chinese Army appears to out-
number the Indian Army by about five to one, a switch to a
nuclear strategy with all the perils this would involve makes
little military sense. Of course, these qualifications apply only
to a fairly low grade Chinese nuclear weapons force. If the day
comes when the country can put a large number of varied
weapons into reliable delivery systems able to do the job
required of them, it will presumably have as valid a military
force as the Russians or Americans.

Against this background, it is possible to trace what evidence
there is about the development of military doctrine among the
military and political authorities of China since the Communists came to power in 1949.[1] Little theory emerged from the
new Government in the period up to 1954 when the Russians
were working their way towards a coherent military doctrine
which would take account of the American heavy nuclear force.
The failure of the United States to use its nuclear weapons in
Korea probably encouraged military orthodoxy which regarded

[1] This subject is covered with exceptional skill in 'Communist
China and Nuclear Warfare', *China Quarterly*, April–June 1960
and in 'Chinese Genie: Peking's Role in the Nuclear Test Ban
Negotiations', The Rand Corporation, June 20th, 1960, both by
Alice Langley Hsieh.

them as prestige or terror weapons which could not be effective against the methods and training of the People's Liberation Army. Following the clear Russian recognition of United States nuclear superiority in 1954, the Chinese Government had to digest the implications of the Dulles threat of atomic retaliation issued on March 8th, 1955. It was in this period that the first serious discussion of nuclear weapons was observed in China. Public statements encouraged the agreeable vision of a nuclear war in which capitalism perished but socialism survived while the United States was accused of using nuclear weapons to stop the liberation of Formosa. Future wars began to be forecast in the light of nuclear weapons. An example of this is the statement made on July 21st, 1955, by Marshal Liu Po-ch'eng:[1]

> With the emergence of atomic weapons and jet weapons [he said], military science has registered a new development. It is anticipated that war in the future will be a combined operation by the land forces, naval forces, air forces, parachutists, and air defence units carried out on the land, at sea, and in the air. The extent of the fronts, the size of the armies, and the use of material supplies will all be greater than heretofore.

In this period, China was relying on Russia for modern and sophisticated equipment. The Peking reactor was being built at this time and so were such things as the production lines for Russian interceptors. Towards the end of 1957, however, a new era seems to have begun in Russian military thought. The inter-continental rocket in August and the *Sputnik* in October were followed, if accidentally, by the Rapacki Plan and the first proposal for an Asian nuclear free zone. Many reasons may be given for the Russian support of these, but one obvious explanation is a desire to find some alternative to offer Communist countries who were asking for Russian nuclear weapons. The Mao-Khrushchev discussions in November, 1957, may well have been the occasion of strong Chinese demands for nuclear support and may have made clear the Russian Government's anxiety not to extend it to a really ambitious Chinese

[1] Report of the First National People's Congress, *Current Background*, No. 347, August 23rd, 1955.

policy. Some support for the idea came from Peking, but not
for some months. Mr. Chou En-lai described the idea on
February 10th, 1958[1] as 'what the Chinese people have all
along supported' (though this was the first mention of such
support), and General Kuo Mo-jo said on March 5th that an
atom-free zone would rule out U.S. bases.[2] By May, the talk of
the atom-free zone was dying away and it was in that month
that the firmest forecast of a Chinese nuclear weapons programme was made by the Commander of the Air Force, Liu
Ya-lou, who wrote 'China's working class and scientists will
certainly be able to make the most up-to-date aircraft and
atomic bombs in the not distant future. By that time, in
addition to the political factor in which we always occupy an
absolutely predominant position, we can use atomic weapons
and rockets . . . in coping with the enemies who dare to invade
our country and undermine world peace. By that time, another
new turning-point will probably be reached in the international situation.'[3]

The really interesting thing about this statement is the fact
that it was made in the heyday of the Great Leap when
communism itself was being promised 'in the not far distant
future.' Since there is no evidence that the same thing has
been said in the more recent period of relative realism, it can
be regarded as merely a general statement of intention. The
phrase 'in the not distant future' may since have been re-
gretted.

The wording and timing of the statement also suggest that
the Chinese Government had made up its mind that self-
sufficiency was the only way and that this would produce a
'turning point' at which the true importance of China would
have to be recognised. What, one may ask, would China's
working class and scientists matter if Russian technical
achievements were available to the People's Liberation Army?

---

[1] New China News Agency, Peking, February 11th, quoted in A.
L. Hsieh 'The Chinese Genie', op. cit. p. 7.
[2] 'Shih-chieh Chih-shih', April 5th, 1958.
[3] 'Seriously Study Mao Tse-tung's Military Thinking', *Liberation Army Newspaper*, May 23rd, 1958, quoted in 'Survey of the
China Mainland Press', No. 1900, November 24th, 1958.

But self-sufficiency could be achieved in one of two ways: by giving the needs of the military a high priority or by broadening and strengthening the whole economic base and building power on that. The real question is the priority which was given to the advanced weapons programme and, in particular, to nuclear weapons. Certainly there is evidence that the military high command was discontented by the use which was being made of the army itself for economic construction. Marshal Lin Piao, the Minister of National Defence, was quoted as saying that the man remained the important factor in modern warfare but that China needed a standing army with modern technical equipment.[1] This might mean a fighter with as good a missile as Chiang Kai-shek's *Sidewinders* or it might mean an urgent requirement for nuclear weapons. It certainly indicated that China is not going to rely forever on 2,500,000 men with little heavy equipment to give them firepower.

The atom-free zone raised its head again in 1959, once more on Russian initiative. In surprisingly strong language, Mr. Khrushchev said in his opening address to the 21st Congress of the Communist Party that 'a zone of peace, above all, an atom-free zone can, and must be created in the Far East and the entire Pacific basin.'[2] The Chinese press referred only to the 'zone of peace' and the idea was not taken up by Chou En-lai when he spoke to the Congress. Mild Chinese press support was given a month later, but it seems fairly obvious that the Russians did not consult the Chinese—presumably because they did not expect them to agree. At the National People's Congress in April, Chou En-lai condemned the arrival of American nuclear and rocket weapons in South Korea and said: 'We advocate the establishment of an area free of atomic weapons, an area of peace, throughout the whole of East Asia and the Pacific region.' The use of the phrase 'East Asia' was original. It presumably covers the string of islands, including Japan, which is friendly to the United States, and even Korea and part of the Chinese mainland; but it could be expected to leave out much of China.

[1] New China News Agency, September 29th, 1959.
[2] *Pravda*, January 28th, 1959.

This effort at dissociation was reaffirmed by the Chinese statements made at the time when an agreement to abolish nuclear tests seemed a serious possibility. The Chinese Government repeatedly said that it could be bound by no agreement to which it was not a party. Russian ideas of general disarmament have been treated sceptically and it has been made clear that negotiations with those who do not recognise China are out of the question.

We may thus conclude that the Chinese Government intends ultimately to have herself counted among the great powers and will create the weapons base to make this possible. It will resist any agreement, such as a test ban, which will put it permanently into an inferior position. The issue really is whether the Chinese Government believes (as official opinion in the West appears to think) that one or two nuclear explosions would strengthen its military position and prestige. Close study of the position shows that there are good reasons for holding back until the nation has the industrial base to make nuclear weapons systems able to do a military job. Which view is dominant is an unresolved issue for the political psychologist.

Chapter 8

India

IN technical terms, India and Canada are undoubtedly the two countries which are most ready to become nuclear powers. They are also the two countries which have been most unqualified in their rejection of nuclear weapons. India has gone even farther than Canada in this respect and has maintained a stern anti-nuclear line in international affairs. The Indian Government pushed the idea of a ban on nuclear weapons tests long before it became fashionable among the great powers as a first step in disarmament; and it has been ready and anxious to proclaim its own non-nuclear status as its atomic energy programme has begun to yield a serious option on a bomb. The sceptic about Indian sincerity in these protestations may point to two tendencies of Indian policy: the high priority given to the atomic energy programme based on complete self-sufficiency in all the related technologies; and the consistent opposition of the Indian Government in the International Atomic Energy Agency to safeguards in peaceful nuclear sharing. These certainly suggest an anxiety to have the option on producing a bomb. There is at present, however, no evidence that this option is being taken up.

The progress of India in the necessary fundamentals of nuclear power has been particularly striking since 1955. In the period between 1955 and 1960, she began the steady creation of a self-sufficient nuclear base which, with extensive Canadian and British co-operation, is now fully established. The programme has been under the direct supervision of the Prime Minister, Mr. Nehru, who is Minister of Atomic Energy. The Department of Atomic Energy has as its Secretary Dr. Homi J. Bhabha, who is also Director of the Atomic Energy Establishment, Trombay, the Chairman of the Advisory Atomic Energy Commission and the Director of the Tata Institute for Fundamental Research.

Dr. Bhabha has obviously been given a high priority in his demands on the scarce skilled manpower resources of India and he has also been allowed generous quantities of money. Although this has attracted press criticism, the Government has no intention of restricting him.

Plans for nuclear development have been coloured by the fact that the country possesses large deposits of thorium. It is estimated that on the Kerala Coast, on the southwest coast of Madras State and in the large deposits in Bihar there are 500,000 tons of thorium—at least half the known world supply. Thorium production at Trombay began in 1955 and in 1956 the decision was taken to put up a uranium refinery to purify the uranium fluoride which was being accumulated. This coincided with the first stage of the Indian reactor programme; and the urgency with which the construction of this facility was carried through showed the anxiety of the Government not to have to rely on foreign supplies of uranium. The first ingot of natural uranium was produced on January 30th, 1959; and in 1961 the plant was producing 30 tons of uranium a year and was being expanded to produce 100 tons. This would enable it to feed the requirements of the existing experimental reactor programme up to and including the first power reactor which is supposed to go into operation in 1965. A large scale leaching plant capable of producing 250 tons of uranium concentrates (equivalent to 200 tons of uranium metal) is expected to be put up in 1962 or 1963.

The next requirement was a plant for the fabrication of fuel elements for reactors. Laboratory studies began in 1956 and Atomic Energy of Canada Limited made information available which allowed a plant to be designed and construction to begin in November, 1957. A fuel element was turned out on June 15th, 1959, and it is confidently claimed by the Head of the Metallurgy Division at Trombay, Brahm Prakash, that this was the first fuel element for an atomic reactor to be produced in Asia outside the Soviet Union. As a matter of policy, all the most sophisticated equipment was constructed in the Trombay Establishment itself—a policy which has been maintained, in spite of the cost, throughout the whole Indian atomic programme.

Three research reactors have also been built at Trombay. The first, known as APSARA, was the first reactor to go into operation in Asia outside the U.S.S.R. when it became critical in August, 1956. It uses enriched uranium supplied by the United Kingdom A.E.A. and is in the one megawatt (thermal) category. The interest in it is chiefly the early date at which Trombay was dealing with a working reactor which had been designed and constructed by Indians. Demand has been strong for its services both in research and in isotope production; and later in 1958 it was put on continuous operation.

The second reactor to be built in India was the Canada India Reactor (known as CIR), which, with 40 megawatts of thermal power, was the first major international atomic project anywhere in the world. Canada offered India a version of her NRX reactor under the Colombo Plan on the general understanding (drawn up in a brief inter-governmental agreement) that costs in India would be paid by the Indian Government and all other costs would be paid by Canada. This has resulted in an approximately equal division of the cost of about 18 million dollars. The reactor became critical on July 10th, 1960. It uses natural uranium with heavy water as a moderator and incorporates the experience gained from long operation of NRX at Chalk River. To meet specific Indian requirements, it has a ring of holes for irradiating thorium and modifications to meet the different geographical conditions of Bombay, with its hot climate and salt water.

Like NRX, it produces no power, but it gives Trombay a really substantial experimental facility and a growing stock of unseparated plutonium. Once it is working continuously at full power, its fuel elements should be able to yield up to eight kilograms of plutonium a year. Since the Canadians have imposed no effective safeguards, this could be used by the Indian Government to provide the fissile material for two or three bombs a year if it chose to run the reactor primarily for the production of weapons grade plutonium. Half the fuel elements for the first charge in CIR were provided by each government, though by straining its resources the Trombay establishment could have provided the entire charge. Canada has in fact provided the second charge under the Colombo

Plan. Since the A.E.E. was aiming for self-sufficiency, it may be assumed that it is accumulating a considerable surplus of natural uranium rods for use in later reactors.

The third Indian research reactor, ZERLINA, was entirely designed and built at Trombay. It is in a very low power category (100 watts) and is being used to examine a large number of combinations of fuels and moderators.

With the object of freeing India from dependence on American or Norwegian production of heavy water, a considerable effort is being made to create heavy water production facilities in the country itself. This is linked to a growing fertilizer industry. The first plant, the Nangal Heavy Water Plant, will be producing at a rate of 15 tons a year early in 1962 and it is hoped to quadruple this by comparatively small modifications which have been developed at Trombay. A second plant, combined with another fertilizer plant, is due to be built at Trombay, where a reconcentration plant for the used heavy water from CIR and ZERLINA is already in operation.

The future reactor programme is moving over from experiment to power production. In mid-1958, the Planning Commission approved the inclusion of an atomic power station in the power development programme of the Third Five Year Plan. Tenders were invited and received from the main nuclear power producing countries for a 300 mW.(e) station (made up of two reactors of equal capacity) to be installed at Tarapur, 62 miles north of Bombay. It is planned that the two reactors will go into operation in the course of 1965, but this is now unlikely.

From the point of view of weapons development, though not of power development, there remains an important gap: the chemical separation plant for plutonium which, it will be recalled, delayed the French weapons programme. The construction of a pilot plant at Trombay for this purpose is in fact well under way under the name of Project Phoenix. It is hoped that this will begin the separation of pure fissile plutonium produced in CIR early in 1963. Dr. G. A. Welch, the Head of the Radiochemistry Division, has been loaned by the United Kingdom Atomic Energy Authority under the Technical

Co-operation Scheme of the Colombo Plan. Writing in *Industrial India*[1] he has described the Trombay approach: 'Although general information is available on a number of processes in use in other countries for this purpose, detailed data for an up-to-date process are not available and have been obtained by the Radiochemistry Division which has also tested the use of indigenous materials wherever possible. At present experiments are in hand to gain experience in the production of pure plutonium metal from solutions of its compounds. Although this final stage is being carried out by the same method as that used in Britain, the U.S.A. and France, research work is also in hand to study the chemistry of certain other plutonium compounds which might be intermediates in a new route to the metal, possibly giving a purer product.' An electrical substation of 3,000 KVA capacity has been designed and a special workshop has been put up so that rigorous inspection of workmanship and materials can be maintained. The plant is costing some 3.7 crores (about £2,750,000).

The production of pure fissile plutonium from a plant of this kind is the last major hurdle for a country planning to explode a nuclear device. If the plutonium plant begins its production in January or February, 1963, and if in the meantime the Indian Government thinks it desirable to design such a device, India could produce a nuclear explosion by the middle of 1963—the date which the Americans and Japanese believe is most likely for the first Chinese explosion.

What deductions about Indian intentions can be made from the decisions which have been taken at Trombay? Like the French programme up to 1955, it is a research and development effort intended to create the scientific and technical capacity to produce nuclear power from Indian resources on Indian soil. As with the French, this must at a certain point offer fissile material which could be used in weapons. Before looking at Indian military and political thought, we may regard one decision as significant: the decision to build the plutonium plant at such an early date. The official reason for wanting plutonium is given as follows: 'Plutonium is of great importance to India's atomic energy programme as, in the

[1] Supplement, January, 1961.

three-stage nuclear power programme envisaged, it will be used to breed Uranium 233 from thorium.'[1]

The A.E.E. plans to follow its coming generation of uranium reactors with a generation of plutonium reactors. Thorium will be irradiated constantly in these reactors, as in CIR, and the ultimate object is Uranium 233 reactors producing more U-233 than they consume by the steady irradiation of India's limitless quantities of thorium. But the fact is that the second stage, the plutonium reactors, is still some considerable distance away. Those who argue that India is not interested in bombs justify the plutonium plant by pointing to plans to introduce small quantities of plutonium into CIR and irradiate them over long periods. In this way it is hoped to study the products of plutonium irradiation. A useful research programme of this kind does not, nevertheless, fully explain the speed with which the plutonium plant has been designed and is being constructed. There has not been the same urgency about the study of separation processes for irradiated thorium although these have an equally important bearing on the future of the Indian power programme. Even the process details for this plant have not yet been worked out. Plutonium, though distant in the power programme, has had a high priority.

The most reasonable inference is that Mr. Nehru, advised by Dr. Bhabha, has decided to give the country the option to produce a nuclear device in 1963 in case this should become politically or militarily necessary. The plutonium plant must be built eventually: why not have it at the soonest possible date? The fact that this technical question has been given a military answer is best illustrated by reference to other countries—such as Canada, Germany or Japan—which are more advanced industrially than India and yet have not made the same moves toward nuclear self-sufficiency. Japan is particularly interesting, since it is not only industrially and economically stronger than India but it has no coal and its hydro-electric reserves are nearing exhaustion. Its first nuclear power station at Tokaimura should be in use in 1964 and a second may be ordered within the next year. This puts it ahead of India.

[1] Report of the Department of Atomic Energy, p. 8.

Yet in spite of this, Japan has not as yet begun to build either a fuel element fabrication plant or a chemical processing plant. On economic grounds, the Japanese appear to have decided not to build either until the late 1960s. Seen against the plans of other countries, the Indian programme has an inescapable shape: it suggests clearly that the Indian Government has consciously and intentionally equipped itself with an option to decide to build nuclear weapons. As a result, the choice which is now open to her is undoubtedly the possibility (assuming continued Canadian abstinence) of being the fifth power to explode a nuclear device. Unless the Russians have chosen to give China such a reactor as CIR without strings— a possibility which even those who think the Chinese bomb is imminent consider most unlikely—India must have a decisive advantage. The only advantage which Peking might have over Trombay is a willingness to take chances.

What is even more significant than the mere explosion of a device is the speed with which India's supplies of pure fissile material will build up after the Tarapur power station begins operation provided this can be obtained without safeguards. By 1969, it should be giving up substantial quantities of plutonium; and since India is able to provide the natural uranium fuel, she may be able to go on avoiding controls over the use of the plutonium. Sites are being sought for two other power reactors, one of which may be a copy of the CANDU (Canadian deuterium uranium) power reactor which is an outgrowth of NRX. It is planned to construct a full-scale plutonium plant at a place which will serve them both. Work is also going ahead on a prototype for an Indian-designed power reactor, though not at the highest priority, in the 20 megawatt category (electrical). This will use natural uranium, heavy water as a moderator, and organic coolants which are being studied in ZERLINA.

The Indian programme has unique access to the experience of other countries because of the anxiety of the Commonwealth to advance Indian industry and of the Russians and Americans (to put it at its lowest) to make sure that the other one does not obtain exclusive Indian patronage. It also has some advantages in its relatively small size. Dr. Bhabha's

position is so strong with the Indian Government that pur-
chasing powers have been taken away from Director General
of Supplies and Disposal and vested in a Purchase Division at
Trombay. 'A far reaching delegation of financial and cognate
powers' has also been made to Dr. Bhabha under the advice
(which he may reject) of an Internal Financial Adviser.[1]
Expenditure as officially published—the true figures are considerably higher—rose from 424.28 lakhs (£3,182,100) in
1958–59 to 599.38 lakhs (£4,495,350) in 1960–61 and is rising
at an increasing rate.[2] The manpower strength of the Establishment is also growing rapidly and on December 31st, 1960,
it had 1,275 scientific personnel and 1,048 technical personnel.[3]
There is evidence that the Treasury has tried to defer expenditure on atomic energy in the Third Five Year Plan but has
failed.

The fact that the power programme gives an option on
nuclear weapons has never been hidden in New Delhi. Indeed,
it was used to strengthen the Indian denunciation of the
possession, testing or use of such weapons. It is obviously more
impressive to renounce something which one could possess
comparatively easily than to renounce the unattainable. In an
address to Parliament on February 10th, 1958, the then
President of India, Dr. Prasad, said:

> For ourselves, my Government desire to make it clear be-
> yond all doubt, that while we could, if we so decided, un-
> wisely, produce atomic weapons, with the resources and
> skills that we have and can develop, we have no intention
> whatsoever of acquiring, manufacturing or using such
> weapons or condoning their use by any State. Our endeav-
> ours in the atomic field will remain confined to the peaceful
> use of atomic energy.

This position has been strictly adhered to. It is held so firmly
as the basis of public policy that even officers in the armed
forces hesitate to discuss hypothetical situations in which others

[1] Report of the Department of Atomic Energy, Government of
India, 1960–1, p. 46.
[2] *Ibid.*, p. 47.
[3] *Ibid*, p. 44.

might use them. No instruction is given in the effects of nuclear weapons; and only the practice of using British Staff College notes gives the Indian officer any knowledge of these weapons and the tactics which they impose. The tactics themselves are no part of Indian Army doctrine. Although politically the Praja Socialists and Swatantra parties would favour an alliance with the United States, and the Communists an alliance with the Soviet Union, they seldom if ever mention nuclear weapons. They would only do so to condemn any Indian tendency to think of acquiring them.

The speeches of the Prime Minister, Mr. Nehru, have seldom failed to make reference to India's peaceful intentions in her atomic energy programme and frequently contain unqualified assurances. For example he told the Lok Sabha on May 17th, 1956, when talking of the Canada India Reactor, that India's atomic energy programme would be aimed at the peaceful use of atomic energy. In a speech to the National Development Council on January 14th, 1961, he said: 'Since we are approaching a stage when it is possible for us if we direct our energies to that end, to make atomic nuclear weapons too, in some foreign papers and others there is a slight apprehension that we might do so. I state absolutely that under no circumstances will we do so whatever might happen.' At the inauguration of CIR on January 16th, 1961, he said: 'Fortunately, everyone believes that we stand for peace and if we have developed atomic energy and research facilities it is for the interest of peace and not for any nefarious or destructive designs.' Inaugurating an 'Atoms for Health' exhibition in New Delhi on February 9th, 1961, he said: 'India will use atomic power only for peaceful purposes. The utilisation of atomic energy for peaceful purposes is the modern version of converting a sword into a plough-share. Just like the sword becoming too dangerous for use, atomic energy will have disastrous results if used for warfare.' At a press conference on September 7th, 1961, he said: 'If we are opposed to atomic bombs, hydrogen bombs and all that, that is not a mere empty statement for us to make, because before long we would be in a position, we will have the competence and equipment, to make them. But we deliberately decided not to do it, although probably apart from the big countries, there are only two or three countries which are as advanced in this matter as we are in Europe and Asia. But we have deliberately said we will not do it. In a sense, if you like, we have wasted time. That is to say if we want to do it, we have to do it not now but a year later. But we are not going to do it.'

There may be an element of wishful thinking in all this. There is certainly no element of deception. Officials and military men alike reject nuclear weapons even in the frankest private discussions; so do editors and those who might be considered the leaders of public opinion. Even more than Canada, India considers that her position in the world depends on her reputation for morality in public affairs. While showing a defiant determination to fight if, for example, the Chinese persist in encroachments on Indian soil, the feeling is instinctive that India could not maintain her influence while acquiring nuclear weapons. The profession of war is as highly regarded in India as anywhere and the half million men under arms are selected from millions of possible volunteers; but the faith in troops as defenders of the nation stops short of nuclear weapons—'these horrible things,' as Mr. Nehru has called them.

Before proceeding to look at India's foreign and military policy, some consideration should be given to the sort of delivery system which she might use if she were to develop a bomb. On the whole, the general atmosphere of defence planning in a country such as India is such as to make a sophisticated delivery system appear much less urgent. No very sophisticated defences are expected from possible enemies. When military men are asked what they would do if the country, under some terrible threat, suddenly felt that it must equip itself with a stock of bombs, they generally reply that so appalling a development in international relations would almost certainly make it possible for India to call on one of the existing nuclear powers for assistance. But even if this is ruled out, they do not believe that it would be difficult to find some sort of delivery system. The main striking power of the Indian Air Force at present consists of 58 *Canberra* bombers which they have had since 1958 and handle effectively. This force will probably continue in the front line for some time. For a very distant strike, the country possesses three Boeing 707s and nine Super-Constellations which might possibly be adapted. The Third Five Year Plan provides for the purchase of four additional civil jet aircraft.

A strong trend has developed in defence policy to avoid wherever possible the outright purchase of sophisticated equipment abroad. This is likely to continue and will mean that the Indian armed forces will be slow in re-equipment but will have the back-up inside the country for their tanks and aeroplanes if they find themselves in a drawn-out conflict. This policy is dictated primarily by concern about imposing a permanent burden on the foreign exchange resources of the country; but it also has the considerable advantage economically that the large sums which all countries spend on defence are used in part to fertilise industry (though they also absorb scarce managerial and technical talent). In aircraft, the policy goes back a long way, though the I.A.F. has until recently preferred to rely on licence agreements rather than Indian research and development. Generally these have been with the United Kingdom. The *Vampire* jet fighter was built under licence and after it the Folland *Gnat* light fighter, and the Avro 748 light transport. On the basis of a proposed supersonic development of the Orpheus engine, the Orpheus 12, the Hindustan Aircraft Factory designed an aircraft intended to fly ultimately at Mach 2 (twice the speed of sound) using two of these engines. Professor Kurt Tank, who at Focke-Wolf designed the *Kondor* maritime bomber and the highly successful F.W.190 fighter was brought from Argentina to direct the design of this aircraft, designated the HF-24. The Indian Government has in principle accepted the Russian offer of the VK-7 engine for it. The decision about this aircraft is important for the future of the Indian military weapons industry, because it is likely to take many years to develop and to cost far more than is expected. The experience of the United States, with her century series, Canada with the *Arrow*, France with the *Mirage 3*, Britain with the *Lightning* and Sweden with the *Draken* is unanimous that Mach 2 aircraft are relatively easy to build but very difficult to make into effective operating weapon systems. Everyone in India appears to be underrating the job ahead. The job may take anything up to eight years and £30m. before air force squadrons are ready. At the same time, there is talk of another project for a jet bomber. As long as the HF-24 is under development, this seems unlikely; but the possibility that India will be forced to consider buying a Mach 2 platform which can be used as a bomber or interceptor, like the *Mirage 4* or British TSR-2, should not be ruled out. This could give her a high performance delivery system by about 1967 or 1968.

Ballistic missiles have not crossed anyone's mind in New Delhi and seem to be entirely associated, in political circles at least, with offensive and undesirable forms of warfare. Any attempt to build missiles for nuclear weapons would have to start from nothing and would depend heavily on foreign assistance, particularly in view of the unsophisticated state of Indian electronics. It seems, therefore, that an Indian nuclear weapon would rely mainly on the *Canberra* and (probably towards 1970) its successor.

Can India get along without nuclear weapons? Indian foreign policy recognises two possible enemies: Pakistan and China. The right and the left can be identified by the order in which they are placed—Pakistan first for the left, China first for the right. Mr. Krishna Menon, the Defence Minister, is generally thought to be directing the planning of the armed forces primarily to the possibility of war with Pakistan. Even he, however, is taking vigorous action to build border roads in Ladakh, Sikkim and Assam; and the steady rise in the strength of the armed forces from about 350,000 to figures which are thought to be approaching 500,000 indicate that the Government is addressing itself to the situation to the north where it is militarily inferior as well as that to the west where it is decisively superior.

As far as the Pakistan problem is concerned, there is constant concern at the closeness of Washington's relations with Karachi. The supply of such modern military equipment as the F-104 *Starfighter* is generally accompanied by rumours that the United States Government is toying with the idea of giving Pakistan nuclear weapons. Such an action by a third party is considered to be the only foreseeable way in which Pakistan might acquire these weapons. A national programme by the Pakistanis is ruled out: and in any case it is fairly obvious that by the time this produced any results India's atomic potential will be far greater. This fact in itself is expected to deter Pakistan. As far as Pakistan is concerned, the Indian Government's whole effort is to keep the line to Washington open so that it can stay the hand of the Americans. The Kennedy Administration has shown itself so receptive to the Indian point of view and so unwilling to contemplate any nuclear sharing with its allies that there is little concern at present. Pakistan therefore creates no urge towards Indian acquisition of nuclear weapons. On the other hand, Pakistan's repeated statements that any Indian effort to make a bomb would be an act of aggression and war directed at them, offers one additional (though slight) reason for Indian reluctance to contemplate nuclear weapons.

The situation with regard to China is not quite so simple. Indians must ask three questions. When will they get a bomb? How will it damage India politically? Might it be a direct threat militarily? On the first of these questions, the Indian Government is inclined to accept as uncritically as most western governments the general belief that the Chinese are determined to have a bomb and will make sure they get one at an early date. There is no doubt in New Delhi that both in atomic science and in aircraft they have more resources and more experience than the Chinese—and of course they also have sophisticated foreign patronage. The Indians who attended the opening of the Peking research reactor in 1957 were surprised at how little the Chinese seemed to know about it; and the Russians have expressed the opinion at a high level that Chinese nuclear technology is very primitive and will take until 1970 to produce even a device. Nevertheless, this view has not been accepted by the Prime Minister or the Government. The working assumption in New Delhi is that they must expect a Chinese explosion between 1963 and 1965. Russian aid to China is not ruled out, but it is considered unlikely as long as relations are as bad as they are at present.

According to Mr. Nehru, the Indian Government has not given much thought to the political situation which will be produced by this explosion.[1] The prospect of a battle for prestige being fought out in Asia between a nuclear China and a non-nuclear India does not disturb him. The Indians do not believe that the people of South-East Asia will be particularly frightened by Chinese bomb threats, if only because when it comes to nuclear power the United States will remain overwhelmingly superior to China. The political position is a reflection of the military position; and the Indian Government believes that any use of nuclear weapons by the Chinese must make western nuclear weapons available to India. Curiously those who have thought about it appear to consider this possibility less morally objectionable than an Indian bomb.

In spite of the sense of betrayal and treachery which the Chinese aroused in the border conflict, there is no disposition in New Delhi to regard a Chinese use of nuclear weapons against anyone but the Americans or Chiang Kai-shek as remotely possible. Even a major conventional war is generally ruled out. Mr. Nehru holds the view that neither side could win such a war across the mountains which divide the two countries. Others argue that while India would fight hard and honourably, she could not hope to hold the Chinese by herself; but that in any such conflict she could rely on Russian neutrality and the military support of the rest of the world. The policy of non-alignment has implicit in it a recognition that there are those who would come to India's support with either nuclear or conventional forces if they were asked. The question of credibility (a putative father of any new nuclear weapons programme) is never asked and would not be asked until the distant day when China could strike heavily against North America and Britain.

Non-alignment therefore does not imply non-reliance. The fact that even Russia has refused to back China in her conflict with India is seen as proof of the security which India gets from her policy of rejection of nuclear weapons and good relations with everyone (leaving aside Portugal, South Africa and Pakistan). Going into nuclear weapons would thus, it is argued, weaken her military position as well as her political and moral position.

[1] The *Guardian*, October 23rd, 1961.

It must be assumed that India's option on nuclear weapons will grow cheaper as the years go on and her power programme develops. At present, it is impossible to find anyone in a position of influence or authority who thinks it likely, or even possible, that this option might be taken up.

Chapter 9

Sweden

THE desirability of possessing atomic weapons has dominated discussions of Swedish defence policy since the early fifties, and will continue to do so for many years to come. It is however most unlikely that Sweden will ever take the step of manufacturing atomic weapons for herself, or of accepting them from more powerful nations. For it seems that the military advantages which might be obtained by the possession of atomic weapons, and which are frequently and cogently argued by important sections of Swedish opinion, are outweighed by a sense of the political dangers which atomic weapons would bring with them. At least in its present mood, Swedish foreign policy aims at minimising the hazards of the inevitable international conflicts of interests which exist. Atomic weapons are regarded by the present government as a means by which these hazards would be increased, and it is unlikely that any succeeding government would be able responsibly to persuade itself that the opposite may be true.

Even if this prediction should prove at some point to be inaccurate, however, the balance of argument in Sweden on the possession of atomic weapons has a special interest in studies of the spread of atomic weapons. For Sweden is wedded to a policy of neutrality. Swedes themselves are, indeed, eager to point out that their neutrality is not just a diplomatic posture but a 'way of life'. It is certainly the case that the concept of neutrality is often regarded in Sweden as a desirable end in itself, as democracy is considered to be in the West, for instance.

One immediate and practical consequence of this is, of course, that where the possession of atomic weapons is concerned, Sweden must expect to do everything for herself. Though there have been, on several occasions, suggestions that a decision to equip Swedish defences with atomic weapons might be implemented by obtaining these from abroad, it has always been recognised that neutrality would seem to be compromised if this could not be done on a simple commercial basis, and in particular without the acceptance of conditions of sale which might be interpreted as political commitments by potential enemies. It is also recognised that for the foreseeable future at least, atomic weapons will not be sold on international markets as if they were sacks of wheat, or electronic computers. Therefore Swedes of all shades of opinions have quickly concluded, if with varying degrees of reluctance, that any atomic weapons there may be will have to be made entirely in Sweden. One result is that Sweden is a nation in which the economic and physical difficulties of making atomic weapons apply with almost full rigour.

Technically there would be no insuperable difficulty in the mounting of a Swedish programme for the manufacture of atomic weapons, and indeed the civil atomic power and research programme now under way is sufficiently well-advanced and self-contained to be a sound foundation for a military programme. The Adam reactor being built south of Stockholm will eventually produce some 150,000 kW. of heat, and thus might be made to serve as a source for some 33 kgs. of plutonium every year. The reactor is of unusual design in that it is cooled by heavy water and that its fuel is made of uranium oxide (rather than metal). But the possible commercial disadvantages of this system would not be a handicap because of the shorter irradiation time for military plutonium production required. The construction of a still larger reactor capable of producing more than 1,000,000 kW. of heat has recently (1961) been recommended to the Government, primarily on the grounds that something should be provided for Swedish industry and technology to work upon against the time when atomic power may become a commercially attractive proposition. The likelihood is that this recommendation will be accepted, though the reactor concerned cannot be completed before 1965.

In the meantime Swedish industry is well endowed with facilities for manufacturing fuel elements for atomic reactors from ore which is being mined in two regions on the mainland of Sweden. Whether these ore deposits are adequate to support a military programme is not certain. These facilities would serve as a means of providing the greater quantities of nuclear fuel needed to supply a military production programme, though there is of course no suggestion that they were created for any but strictly civilian purposes. In the supply of technically trained people of the kind needed to staff a military development programme, Sweden is well provided. Indeed a good deal of the country's industrial prosperity rests on advanced metallurgical and electrical engineering, and though a military atomic power programme of any appreciable size would probably be a considerable strain, there would be no absolute shortage of the men and the skills needed for the purpose. Similar considerations would probably attend the financing of a military atomic power programme—for a small nation the cost would seem high, but with some difficulty (and improvisation) it could probably be met. But the creation of an atomic industry able to provide enough tactical atomic weapons—which is urged by some sections of Swedish opinion —would be a comparatively slow process taking the best part of a decade.

As far as the development of the means of delivery for atomic weapons is concerned, the Swedish problem is made much easier by the fact that interest in nuclear weapons is confined to tactical uses. Up to the present, military aircraft production has been concentrated on the *Draken* single seater fighter and the *Lansen* all-weather ground attack aircraft. Missile development has been concentrated on a small air-to-surface powered bomb for use in the *Lansen*, on a naval surface-to-surface missile and a simple surface-to-air missile. As long as there is no need to go great distances, a country which is the home of firms of such high reputation as SAAB and Bofors could probably design and develop an aircraft or missile able to carry atomic weapons in the same time span that would be needed to produce explosives themselves.

The suggestion that atomic weapons would be used—if at all—in tactical deployment appears to run through all Swedish thinking on the subject. The notion that bombs might be used as deterrent instruments to forestall rather than to repulse military attack appears not to be seriously considered. Such a policy, it is argued, would merely invite overwhelming retaliation. There appears to be no trace in Sweden of the doctrine often advanced in France—that a nation's deterrent strength should be matched to its own size and not to that of likely enemies.

By contrast there is no shortage of advocates for the tactical use of atomic weapons. The armed services in Sweden believe that the defence even of a neutral country should rest on atomic weapons. It was a military group which in 1954 first publicly urged that Sweden should obtain them. In this and in other connections, the military in Sweden have drawn support from the increasing reliance of the United Kingdom on atomic weapons, as expounded in successive Defence White Papers. It has proved difficult to maintain the regular forces at their full strength, so that the possible economies of manpower which atomic weapons promise have often been urged as important advantages. A variant of this argument is the suggestion that a small force whose fire-power derives from atomic weapons can be mobilized more quickly, and can thus react more promptly than a larger force based on conventional arms.

But the basic argument of the Swedish military is that atomic weapons are a necessary means of defence primarily because of their great power. Modern armies need modern weapons, the saying goes. More specifically, the argument is advanced that atomic weapons used defensively could inhibit armed invasion by making it possible to destroy supply ports and communications; that seaborne invasion or blockade might be prevented by the same means, and that in the conduct of military operations on the ground atomic weapons would force an enemy to deploy his most powerful forces. One version of the last of these arguments takes the form that Swedish failure to possess atomic weapons would enable an enemy to concentrate his troops as in conventional warfare and thus to establish an advantage over the defending army, whose forces would have to be deployed in the dispersed formations needed to meet attack with atomic weapons.

The purely military case for the possession of atomic weapons is often harnessed to more general considerations,

SWEDEN   155

among which is commonly to be found the assertion that the
Swedish population will defend itself more willingly if it knows
that its military equipment is not wholly outmoded by that of
its enemies. The starting point for this argument is to be found
in the results of a number of public opinion polls carried out in
the last two or three years. At various times these have suggested that Swedish public opinion considers the chances of
defending Sweden to be small unless its armies are equipped
with atomic weapons; other polls have shown that the population appears to consider the chances of successful defence
to be small in any case. Though there is no reason to believe
that conclusions of this kind are an objective measure of a
nation's will to maintain its own defence, and though the
difficulties of recruiting to the armed services are no greater in
Sweden than in other European countries, the fact that Sweden
has undertaken a more comprehensive programme of civil
defence than any other nation in the world is possibly a
measure of the extent to which the morale of a strategically
isolated nation must be supported in circumstances where
nuclear attacks are to be feared.

The military case for atomic weapons dates back to the
presentation in 1954 of a report on the military needs of the
country which was prepared by General Svedlund, the then
Commander-in-Chief. The case was not accepted by the
government, which postponed a decision on the matter. Support for the military case came quickly from the Conservative
Party in Sweden, which was (and is) the largest party in the
Swedish opposition to the Social-Democrat government. This
polarisation now appears to have become permanent, and the
Conservative party has become the chief and the most constant
political advocate of the military need for atomic weapons. By
contrast the Liberal party is divided on the issue. Within the
Social-Democratic party there appears also to be a small but
influential body of opinion which holds that the needs of
modern defence require that Sweden should be equipped with
atomic weapons.

It is worth noting that one component of the political
argument for the possession of atomic weapons is the suggestion that these sharpen a nation's image in the world, and so

enable it to make its voice heard in the making of international decisions. A nation without atomic weapons is a nation without influence, even where its own interests are concerned. And— the argument goes—even a nation committed to neutrality needs to make this known forcefully, so that guileful aggressors shall not be tempted to make inroads on that neutrality. It is only fair to remember that this point of view, important though it may be, is not a dominant part of the Conservative party's case for atomic weapons.

The evolution of the balance between the opposing factions both between parties and within them is likely to be a slow process in Sweden. A hint of what is in store is provided by the report of a study group of eighteen experts established in 1958 by the Social-Democrat party. Though the pros and cons of Swedish possession of atomic weapons were carefully examined in this document, the Congress of the party in 1960 resolved that a decision on the possession of atomic weapons should be postponed until 1964. This decision has no practical effect, for Swedish capacity to make military plutonium would not be sufficient to support a military programme until that date, but it is more important as an indicator of the Government's unwillingness to commit itself to a programme of military production, or even to take an option on the manufacture of atomic weapons at some time in the future.

Indeed the dominant forces within the Government, and particularly the Foreign Ministry, appear to emphasize the political advantages to be obtained by avoiding the manufacture of atomic weapons. Their strongest argument is that Sweden has most to gain from the conclusion of some disarmament agreement between the major powers including a limitation on the development or the manufacture of atomic weapons. Between 1958 and 1961 Sweden's ministers set great store by the negotiations for a test-ban treaty and argued publicly that a Swedish decision to manufacture weapons might jeopardise the success of these negotiations. Speaking of this series of negotiations at the beginning of 1961 the Swedish Prime Minister, Mr. Erlander, said 'if there is no agreement, then we have free hands'.

Accompanying this attitude towards nuclear weapons has

been the intermittent search for devices which would make it practicable for a large tract of northern Europe to dispense with nuclear weapons. While this notion has been raised on several occasions within the Social Democratic party, it received its most dramatic presentation last year when the Foreign Minister, Mr. Undén, proposed at the 1961 General Assembly of the U.N. that there should be created a nuclear-free zone in northern Europe. The proposal now rests with the U.N. Secretariat, which has the task of inviting comments on the proposal from potentially interested nations. The Swedish Government does not apparently consider that it is bound to accede to its own proposal without making conditions which would satisfy its other political ends; and since it would always be possible to require that Russian accession would be a condition for Swedish signature, it is plain that the degree of reality in the proposal is as yet a matter for negotiation. This does not, however, diminish the importance of Mr. Undén's initiative as an indication of the Swedish Government's uneasiness about the distribution of atomic weapons in Europe.

The Undén proposal is also an indication of the processes by which policy about atomic weapons is formed within the Swedish Government. The point here is that the proposal was apparently made without significant discussion in advance within the Cabinet. Because it came when tension was at its height as a result of the Soviet demand for consultations with Finland under the terms of the 1948 Russo-Finnish Treaty, it has been suggested by his critics that Mr. Undén's proposal was intended as a conciliatory gesture towards the Soviet Union. Even if this reading of events were correct, the fact remains that Swedish policy is still against the possession of nuclear weapons. But it is much more likely that Swedish motives in this matter were guided by the simpler wish to ease tension by means of a constructive proposal and, in the process, to enhance Swedish reputations as peacemongers.

This does not imply, however, that Sweden is indifferent to the balance of power between East and West in the parts of Europe bordering the Baltic. Rather the reverse is true. The Government appears to believe that the growth of West German military strength in the Baltic must apparently evoke some kind of Soviet reaction (typified, perhaps, by the Russian interchange with Finland in November 1961). This, the argument goes, increases international tension in the Baltic, and increases the threats to Swedish (and Finnish) neutrality. A corollary to this argument is the commonly held view that Swedish possession of atomic weapons would serve as a spur to manufacture of these devices in the Federal Republic of Germany and would thus precipitate a sequence of threatening military dispositions in and around the Baltic.

The unwillingness of the present Government to manufacture atomic weapons also stems from cogent military arguments, at the strategic as well as the technical level. It is argued that the circumstances in which the military foresee the need of tactical nuclear weapons are unlikely to arise in any foreseeable conflict. It is improbable that a direct attack on the country would be made by conventional armies or navies, so the argument goes, while atomic weapons would be of little value in containing frontier troubles in the far north of Sweden. In terms of strategic attack, an adversary would have to recognise that the Great Powers would consider their interests to be affected by any substantial change of power balance in the Baltic, so that the fact that Sweden possessed atomic weapons would be no guarantee that it would not be conquered.

The special relationship between Sweden and Finland also colours Swedish views on the desirability of atomic weapons. For a number of reasons, mainly historical or born out of the common strategic isolation of the two countries, Sweden acts as if it is obliged to protect the interests of her smaller neighbour, if necessary by military means but certainly by refraining from policies which might seem to disturb the neutrality of the eastern Baltic. It is in this connection that the Swedish Government tends to argue that the possession of atomic weapons might undermine the safety of Finland. Though in one sense this argument is but an illustration of how the presence of great powers can make itself felt at a distance, the sensitiveness which Sweden exhibits to the pressures imposed on Finland is likely to remain an important part of the Swedish attitude towards atomic weapons. In general a consideration for Finland in this sense will tend to inhibit Sweden from the manufacture of atomic weapons.

A still less tangible but equally potent consideration is the belief that Sweden is culturally and by political instinct at one with the West. There is an underlying assumption that in an emergency Sweden could rely on military support from the strategic forces of the West as a whole. Naturally enough this belief tends to sap Swedish resolve to manufacture atomic weapons. It is curious that the argument should be as apparent as it is in a country linked to the West by the most informal ties, when nations like France formally bound to the West by alliances are more ready to assume that serious military threats might have to be met with indigenous strength alone. Perhaps it is that in these matters nations suit their courage to their strength.

Powerful though the groups may be which urge the need of atomic weapons in Sweden, there seems very little doubt that the Social-Democratic party, which has dominated and governed Sweden for nearly a quarter of a century will remain influenced by the political arguments which suggest that the possession of atomic weapons would work against Sweden's real interests. Accordingly the chances are that so long as the party remains in power, Sweden will not manufacture atomic weapons for herself. Nor does it appear that popular demand for atomic weapons is strong enough to make the question into a dominant electoral issue. And in any case it is probable that if the Conservative party gained power in Sweden, it would also be more impressed by the arguments which have so far prevented Sweden from making atomic weapons than it has been as a long frustrated opposition party. Though there is no end in sight to the heart-searching which has occupied Sweden for nearly a decade now, there is no reason to think that the balance of argument will shift decisively in favour of making atomic weapons.

Chapter 10

Switzerland

IF Switzerland should ever manufacture nuclear weapons, this will be properly regarded as a proof that they have not merely come to stay, but that they are likely to become as commonplace in national armouries as are automatic rifles and armoured cars. For Switzerland is a small nation: its area is merely twice that of Wales, as is its population; a dozen cities in the world contain more people than live and work in it; and its national revenue is roughly twice the annual income of the London County Council. That the manufacture of nuclear weapons can be a living and a real issue in such a comparatively small nation state is itself striking evidence of the extent to which they have ceased to be the preoccupation only of the greatest powers. But Switzerland could not carry through a programme for manufacturing its own nuclear weapons for several years. The reasons for believing this will be explored below. It does not follow, however, that the public debate which has been conducted with increasing vigour for the last four years is academic. For one thing, it may easily result in a Swiss decision to embark on a nuclear weapons programme, however difficult this may be. Moreover, the nature of the Swiss constitution, and in particular the machinery by which most substantial political decisions are referred to popular vote, means that the arguments for and against nuclear weapons are more publicly and perhaps more clearly displayed in Switzerland than in any other country. Another characteristic of Swiss politics which influences the discussion of a Swiss nuclear strategy is, however, idiosyncratic. For Switzerland is determined, even more strongly than Sweden, on a policy of armed neutrality. The vehemence with which this policy, and the strategy which it implies, is often advocated as the only means of preserving national integrity and the essential character of Swiss life suggests, indeed, that 'belligerent neutrality' would be a more appropriate name. All sections of Swiss opinion accept the traditional reliance of Swiss military policies on the most modern of available weapons.

It is not therefore surprising that the first mention of nuclear weapons for Switzerland should have come from Swiss strategists. They have advocated the virtues of nuclear weapons since the early fifties, almost exclusively on account of their potential tactical role in the repulse of land attacks on Switzerland. The timing of these overtures to the public debate still under way is significant on two counts. This was the period in which the tactical usefulness of nuclear weapons was first suggested in the United States. The early fifties also saw the substantial recasting of traditional Swiss defence strategy, and the abandonment of the idea that the integrity of the state could be preserved by means of a retreat on the mountain redoubt in the heart of the country. Present policies are directed towards the halting of possible attacks as near as possible to the national frontiers. This is in part inspired by a consideration of the direction and the objectives of the most likely attacker (universally assumed to be the Soviet Union). Some weight has also been given to the argument that anything less than a defence at the frontiers might be considered to be a modification of neutrality, for it would enable nations concerned only with such military prizes as the right of passage through Swiss territory to assume this right with comparative impunity.

The decision to defend the Swiss lowlands in strength and with determination naturally set in train requirements for weapons not previously employed in Swiss defences, and the Swiss Government embarked in 1954 on a programme of equipping the Swiss army with heavy tanks. This innovation was based on a calculation by the Army that these vehicles were a necessary defence against mobile columns wishing to move through the Swiss lowlands. Opponents of the plan argued that anti-tank guns would be equally effective and more obviously in accord with the international policies of a nation determined never to be a military aggressor. The usefulness of nuclear weapons suggested itself in this debate as a further means for the defence of the frontiers, and in this context the matter was raised in the Federal Assembly, the

Federal Council (or elected Cabinet) and throughout influential public opinion, military and civilian.

The result is that the uses to which nuclear weapons would
be put in potential wars have been spelled out in some detail
by those who advocate their employment in the national
defence. It is foreseen that nuclear weapons might be used to
destroy or to break up concentrations of hostile troops moving
towards and across the frontiers, or to make 'interdiction'
attacks on supply points and communications used by a hostile
power or to put anti-aircraft missiles out of action. The
possibility that nuclear weapons might be used to lay a curtain
of radio-active pollution along the frontiers was once current,
but appears to have disappeared from professional thinking on
the subject. The unpredictability of warfare is also emphasised
in military circles, and it is argued that it cannot be foretold
exactly how an army or an air force will need to make use of
the most advanced weapons in its armoury.

In political circles, arguments of a more strategic flavour
have been debated. Thus it is argued that the possession of
nuclear weapons brings stability to international relations—a
version of the argument with which an independent nuclear
striking force has usually been justified by French strategists.
This presupposes, of course, some means of delivering the
weapons against targets in the heartland of potential enemies,
and is, for this reason, more out of touch with Switzerland's
technical possibilities of the next few years than the arguments
for tactical nuclear weapons. A more realistic doctrine has
been enunciated by those who admit that Switzerland would
not ordinarily be considered as a military prize in its own
right, but merely as a means to an end—a means by which
conventional forces might outflank natural obstacles such as
the Rhine. In these circumstances, it is argued, the possession
of nuclear weapons would certainly make a would-be violator
of Swiss integrity think twice. The culmination of these arguments lay in the declaration of the Federal Council of July
11th, 1958, that 'our Army must be provided with the most
effective weapons for the preservation of our independence and
the protection of our neutrality. Among these are atomic
weapons.'

The question of nuclear weapons has been a subject of parliamentary discussion since 1955. The policy issue has been sharpened in Switzerland since the Hungarian revolution in 1956, partly because this was a reminder of the proximity of trouble, and partly as a consequence of the important part played by the Swiss (and especially by the German-speaking part of the population) in the resettlement of large numbers of Hungarian refugees. However, opposition to Swiss nuclear weapons also began to coalesce during 1957, and in the following year a left-wing movement within the Social Democratic Party attempted to work out a policy that would isolate the nation from nuclear defence. Since then informal groups (with a composition similar to the Campaign for Nuclear Disarmament in the United Kingdom) have sought—as Swiss electoral procedures permit—to amend the constitution so as to outlaw nuclear weapons. This proposal is to be voted on in a referendum on April 1st, 1962, and will most probably be defeated.[1] Though it is opposed to this attempt to make the possession of nuclear weapons unconstitutional, the Social Democratic Party is committed to a policy which demands that any decision to embark on a nuclear weapons programme should be submitted to popular referendum. The present position is that technical studies of the uses to be made of nuclear weapons and of the feasibility of making them are continuing within the Swiss military staff. A final political decision by the Government would not be taken until a positive recommendation to manufacture nuclear weapons, and a prescription as to how this might be accomplished, had been submitted by the military. Given the comparative openness of Swiss policy-making, military as well as civilian, it is probable that the military recommendation would be based strictly on technical and military considerations, and not on an assessment of the political difficulty of carrying it out.

The likely defeat of the constitutional amendment in the popular referendum is a mark of the extent to which Swiss public opinion accepts that neutrality may have to be defended in the most powerful manner possible. Many who do not at

[1] The proposal was defeated.

present consider that Swiss defence should be based on nuclear weapons are eager not to tie their army's hands in the future. There appears also to be a considerable feeling of national pride that Swiss forces have, for decades, been equipped with the 'best' or most 'modern' weapons, and a suggestion that a nation which has kept up with much larger ones in the quality of its manufactures or of its currency should not deny itself the weapons which the most powerful nations consider to be necessary in the modern world. This is a somewhat unexpected illustration of the way in which considerations of national prestige may play an important part even in the formation of policy in nations which eschew direct influence on international relations.

A curious feature of the balance of public opinion about nuclear weapons is the apparently clear division on cultural lines. It appears that a majority of German-speaking Swiss would be in favour of the manufacture of nuclear weapons as soon as this could be arranged, while French-speaking Swiss seem to be more inclined to argue for a postponement of the decision. Such a cleavage of Swiss public opinion is not unusual. In its present form it appears to be linked with the German-speaking population's opposition to trade relaxation with the Soviet bloc. The sharp polarisation of Swiss opinion along these lines necessarily increases the difficulty of knowing how the argument will eventually be resolved. The same cleavage also enhances the extent to which internal dissension would be increased and embittered if the Government were to attempt to carry through a programme for making nuclear weapons. A prudent government would seek to postpone such a step until the public debate has further clarified the issues.

The opponents of American nuclear weapons manufacture criticise the military case for nuclear weapons on the grounds that it exaggerates the capability of the weapons or that it predicates circumstances which are unlikely to occur. These criticisms are particularly well-informed in Switzerland, where the army is largely based on part-time but continuing civilian service. The argument that unforeseen uses for nuclear weapons may arise seems to take priority over detailed military criticisms, such as the difficulty of attacking targets even on the frontiers without endangering substantial numbers of the Swiss population.

The view that nuclear weapons are incompatible with neutrality dominates the belief—current in the Social Democratic Party, for instance—that nuclear policies would endanger neutrality because they could only be effective with the implicit nuclear protection of some more powerful nation. There is some reason to think that the opposition to nuclear weapons might disappear if the possession of tactical nuclear weapons became common in other nations. Curiously enough, however, this susceptibility of Swiss opinion to decisions of other nations is not matched by a belief that Swiss policies should be formulated so as to avoid undesirable results abroad. Certainly the argument appears to be rare that Switzerland should do without nuclear weapons so as not to incite other nations (such as Germany) to the possession of such weapons. A more effective and more common criticism of the movement to mount nuclear policies in Switzerland is the argument that it is inconceivable that there could be a serious military attack on the nation without accompanying conflagration in Western Europe, and that—as a consequence—the integrity of Switzerland can only be secured by the forces which tend to keep the peace in Europe and, in particular, by the balance of mutual deterrence between East and West. It follows—the argument goes—that Swiss nuclear weapons are at best unnecessary, and may even be inflammatory.

It is of course impossible to predict how the balance will in the end be struck between the advocates of nuclear weapons and their opponents. A decision to make them will only result from an open and public debate and it will be surprising if there is an attempt by the Government to force a decision before the end of 1963. In practice, of course, it does not follow that a decision that nuclear weapons would be desirable could be followed by a practical plan for going ahead. There is no doubt that in Switzerland independent manufacture would be a considerable strain. For though the nation is well-provided with technological skills of the highest quality, the numbers of men necessary to mount a nuclear weapons programme could only be recruited with great difficulty, and at the expense of other industrially important enterprises. This restriction, it is true, will be eased in important ways with time and with the growth of the civilian nuclear power industry.

At present the national nuclear energy centre is equipped with two research reactors—one of them of unusual design—and a small power reactor (150,000 kW.) is under construction. These installations are however strictly controlled by means of a bilateral agreement with the United States (which is supplying fuel) with the result that the reactors could only assist a military programme by training men in the operation of reactors.

The difficulty presented by the scale of the process of weapons manufacture is, however, less immediately acute than two other technical problems. In spite of extensive prospecting, appreciable amounts of uranium have not so far been found within the territory of Switzerland. To be sure there is uranium in plenty in the Alps, but in such low concentrations that its extraction would be prohibitively expensive and difficult. A more recent discovery of coal seams containing uranium in small concentrations is not thought to be a practicable source of the material even though the natural concentration of uranium can easily be increased by burning the coal. On the other hand it is unofficially suggested that the chronic world surplus of uranium must in the long run ensure that uranium will become available without international controls, and there have even been allegations by Swiss that a 'black market' in uranium already exists.

The other great technical difficulty in making nuclear weapons in Switzerland is that of testing bombs. The small size of the country and the high density of the population is an obvious drawback. There is a body of scientific opinion which holds that it would not be safe to test bombs in tunnels in the Alps because of the likelihood that these would set off destructive avalanches and landslides.

So far as the manufacture of nuclear explosives is concerned, it is therefore likely that the process would be difficult and time-consuming in Switzerland. It is most unlikely that—with her own resources—the nation could equip itself with anything like an adequate tactical nuclear force in less than a decade. On this time-scale the problems of providing tactical delivery systems would be less burdensome, for the techniques already exist for developing aircraft or missiles of the types necessary to deliver nuclear warheads over ranges of the order of fifty miles.

Chapter 11
Israel

THE case of Israel is a special one in almost every way. She has been technically at war with her neighbours since the State was founded in 1947. Although her population is only 2,200,000, she has a scientific capacity which is potentially comparable with the larger middle powers, such as Canada or India, and a technology which is noted for its innovation and originality. Politically, Israel has never found a comfortable place in the East-West dialogue. Russia disdains her and supports the Arab countries in their desire to destroy her; the United States and Britain are embarassed by Israel—though they grudgingly and with as little publicity as possible let her have enough military equipment to hold the balance with the Arab countries; France offers her something like a genuine military alliance, but in spite of President de Gaulle's assurances it is feared that this will not outlast the Algerian war; and even the Afro-Asian world of neutralism provides no haven because the sworn enemies of Israel are prominent among the neutralists.

Israel has come into existence as a state and maintained herself by a thorough mastery of the art of war. Although she might be said to have been born of a United Nations resolution, she owes almost nothing to legality and the comity of nations. Israelis believe, with justice, that if they exist it is because they have put their faith in good troops with high morale and the best possible weapons. Where most of the new countries were created by the legislation of the old colonial powers and have not had their right to exist seriously questioned, Israel fought her way into life and breathes only because her Army is still unchallenged. For her, power and existence are more closely linked than for perhaps any other country on earth. Nuclear weapons, as the most important form of power available to man, may thus appear as the greatest possible guarantee of existence of Israel. Most Israelis believe that the Arab world will stop at nothing to destroy them and they can find ample justification for this view in the broadcasts of Cairo Radio. In general, while they are anxious for peace and good relations, the unspoken assumption of Israeli military policy is that they too must ignore no possibility which can add to their power and security. All military weapons are examined closely and every possibility of development or purchase is carefully watched.

Against this background, it should also be pointed out that secrecy is widely and effectively applied to all subjects in Israel which have military implications. The idea that the country is at war has not been so pervasive since the Sinai Campaign of 1956; but such information as the size of the armed forces or the military budget is still not published. A major effort was made to keep the first nuclear reactor of any size (that at Dimona in the Negev) a complete secret even while extensive construction operations were going on. Various American officials were given, in total, seven different explanations of what the factory was, none of them accurate. An important uncertainty is provided at present by the fact that nothing has been revealed about the sort of arrangements which have been agreed on nuclear matters with France.

In most countries it is possible to have a fairly clear idea of the direction military planning is taking. Israeli policy seems to have a comprehensible direction, but we must constantly recognise a certain truth in the Arab conviction that they are up against a clever and innovating people with a tradition of conspiracy and stealth. If the Israeli Government decided to produce nuclear weapons, it would almost certainly do so in great secrecy and with great resource. There is a certain tendency among the Israelis to encourage this notion as an additional deterrent and as an advertisement to the Arabs that they cannot hope to destroy Israel.

All questions relating to atomic energy have from the earliest days of the State of Israel been subject to the Ministry of Defence. The men who were mainly responsible for nuclear matters between 1949, when the first moves were made, and 1960, were men whose primary interest was chemistry. It has always been said that, in the Weizmann tradition, Israel has been run by chemists; and this is true of the first chairman of the Atomic Energy Commission, Professor Bergman, and the leading figure in the reactor programme, Professor Dostrovsky. The first plans for the creation of a basic nuclear weapons technology were laid soon after the end of hostilities in 1948. At that time, a group of young scientists were brought together under the Ministry of Defence as the Atomic Energy Commission; and, while this body has remained in the general orbit of defence, these men have come to hold powerful positions in Israeli research and science. The six originals—de-Shalit, Yekutieli, Goldring, Talmi, Pelah and Haber-Schaim—were all sent abroad in 1949 to study under the best men in various fields. They went to Holland, Switzerland, Britain and the United States and gradually all six obtained appointments in the United States. During 1953 and 1954 most of them returned to Israel and a nuclear physics division was established in the Weizmann Institute at Rehovoth in the spring of 1954. The department now has 60 members, including students and technicians, and Dr. de-Shalit has risen to be technical director of the Institute. Of the six, only Dr. Haber-Schaim failed to return to Israel from the United States, although the others regularly go abroad for extended periods of study and research.

The research base has constantly expanded and has been helped by the establishment of the first Israeli reactor at Nachal Sorek not far from the Weizmann Institute. The A.E.C.'s policy is to concentrate nuclear development at Nachal Sorek and in the area in the Negev where the second experimental reactor is now under construction and where Israel's only supplies of natural uranium are to be found. As these applied facilities grow up, it is intended to keep the work of the Weizmann Institute more fundamental.

The reactor at Nachal Sorek has a designed rating of five thermal megawatts. Its situation was partly determined by the fact that the water in the area is good and the drainage, in case of accident, is towards the sea. The United States Government contributed $350,000 towards the total cost (which was more than $3,000,000) and supplies a 90 per cent enriched uranium-aluminium alloy under a normal bilateral agreement in which

Israel gets the fuel on loan, pays four per cent on its value, returns it after burn-up and pays for the reduction in U-235 content. In some cases (such as Germany) the Americans have allowed local firms to manufacture the fuel elements, but the Israeli Atomic Energy Establishment did not consider a facility of this kind justified by the needs of Nachal Sorek. The reactor is one of the largest reactors of the swimming pool type, using natural water to cool and moderate. Most of the reactor equipment was bought in the United States and the design of the establishment was shared by Israeli and American architects. In the laboratories and the ancillary equipment, there is not the same evident desire to achieve self-sufficiency which is so marked in India. This may be the difference in mentality between a nation of 400,000,000 people and one of 2,200,000. Where, however, there is a reasonable demand inside the country for a piece of equipment it is developed; and such machines as fast and slow scalers and power supplies at Nachal Sorek have been designed and produced in Israel.

From the weapons point of view, the first Israeli reactor of any interest is the one being built near Dimona, in the Negev. This is rated at 24 megawatts (thermal) and so may be said to be broadly in the same category as the French G-1, the Canadian NRX and the Indian CIR. From the start, as has been noted, the whole operation has been surrounded with secrecy. Many reasons are offered for the refusal to reveal the nature of the building which was going up in the Negev, including the likelihood of sabotage and the inevitability of sensational reports of Israeli bomb development. It may be pointed out, however, that sabotage is avoided by normal military precautions around much more strategic targets (such as electricity generating plants) and secrecy was bound to stimulate the rumours; so one must conclude that the Ministry of Defence intended and still intends to cover the atomic energy programme with its system of blanket security.

Since the revelation in December 1960, that the Dimona project was a nuclear reactor, most of the main facts about it have emerged. It will be fuelled with natural uranium and moderated with heavy water. The A.E.E. investigated a number of possible designs with the leading atomic powers and it was decided to modify the design of the French EL-3 heavy water research reactor being built at Brest to meet Israeli needs. Governments anxious to know Israel's intentions towards nuclear weapons are naturally anxious to know the terms of the agreement with France, but both Tel Aviv and Paris have remained completely silent on this point. It has been suggested in the United States that the French are using the reactor as a source of plutonium for their weapons programme and will provide the fuel and take back the irradiated material for this purpose. This is denied in the most authoritative circles in Israel, where it is said that no commitments of any kind have been made to France. As the reactor is not due to be completed until 1964, no decision, it is said, has yet been taken about fuel. Some people in the Israeli programme appear to believe that it is possible to get natural uranium on the world market without any significant controls over the use of the plutonium which comes out of the reactor. Others argue that this might at any rate be true by 1964. The official view is that this is unlikely and that it will probably be necessary to make an agreement under which the fuel is supplied by one or other of the nuclear powers and brought back to that country for separation. It is also being intimated officially, though no announcement has been made, that no chemical separation plant is contemplated at present. If this is the present situation, the military importance of Dimona is obviously negligible, at least for many years. The weight of evidence is certainly on this side of the argument. Nevertheless, several questions are not being adequately answered. Would a country such as Israel embark on such an expensive project without making some arrangements for the provision of fuel? Why has so much secrecy surrounded every stage of the project? Can one be certain of French intentions towards their friends among possible nuclear powers in view of the French Government's failure to make a clear stand on the sort of sharing it will contemplate?

Like most atomic energy authorities, the A.E.E. in Israel is anxious to establish as much independence as it can. If natural uranium is available without inspection and control, the chances are strong that the Israelis will pay somewhat more to obtain it on this basis. Assuming that there are no French safeguards on the reactor, they could then have a supply of plutonium (Dimona will probably produce 4–6 kilograms a year if operated at full power) which would give them an option on a weapons programme if they were prepared to build a chemical separation plant. If fuel was required without safeguards and could not be found, it would be possible to refine uranium from the phosphates near the Dead Sea; but as this process is estimated to cost more than ten times as much per ton of uranium as the world price, it will only be attractive to the atomic energy authorities if the Cabinet has decided that there is an urgent military requirement.

Heavy water supplies for Dimona are also virtually certain to be imported. Some interest has been shown in a process developed at the Weizmann Institute for the production of heavy water containing the heavier oxygen isotopes which has proved to be economical for reconcentrating heavy water containing heavy hydrogen. It is not apparently a cheap method of producing it. If, therefore, the Israeli Government is planning to use Dimona as the basis for a weapons programme, it will have to obtain fuel and heavy water without strings or produce them at great cost, operate the reactor at high powers and remove the uranium rods at frequent intervals so as to avoid the excessive production of plutonium 240, build a separation plant, and design a bomb. Dimona would probably provide enough plutonium for one bomb a year by 1966. The separation plant would take at least two years to build and enough people are watching for it to make it most unlikely that it could be built secretly in the small area of Israel. Above all, the source which is finally found for the fuel is certain to become public. We may conclude, therefore, that Dimona appears at present to be no part of a bomb programme and that it will be difficult to turn it over to weapons development without this fact becoming obvious.

The future is nevertheless likely to yield a steadily widening base of Israeli self-sufficiency. In the period between 1951 and 1958, the heavy water process has developed along with the techniques needed to extract natural uranium from the phosphates. At the level of research into these chemical processes, there is every sign that the A.E.E. is determined to learn as much as possible and to construct small pilot plants. As far as chemical separation is concerned, one step has been taken in the direction of self-sufficiency in these difficult processes. 'Hot laboratories' for work with irradiated material have been built with British co-operation near the Nachal Sorek reactor. American aid was given in the equipment and the technicians have been British-trained. It would be reasonable to expect a larger development of this kind at a later stage in association with the Dimona reactor.

The speed with which Israel goes into power reactors depends on developments in the economics of nuclear power stations. The country has only a small amount of oil of her own, but is expanding her electricity consumption very rapidly. The existing power stations get almost all their oil from Iran and are being expanded to give 570 mW (e) by 1965 and about 1000 mW. (e) by 1972. The present thinking is that a nuclear reactor should provide 100 mW of the power requirements of 1965–72 stage. A government decision on this is expected during 1962. It is likely that a considerable effort will be made to provide the fuel elements for this reactor from Israeli sources—either by importing ore or by refining the phosphates. Fuel element studies have been done at the Technion, in Haifa, under Dr. Yiftah, who has worked at the Argonne National Laboratory in the United States. A number of people involved in this work have been sent abroad to study and are expected to return in 1962–3. This suggests a time-scale of 1965 or 1966 for beginning work on fuel for a power reactor which might be ready in 1967 or 1968. Before any such plans are approved, however, the question of cost is certain to be argued very strongly. The government will have to decide how anxious it is to maintain and increase its option to obtain a stockpile of weapons grade fissile material. This is essentially a political and military decision.

Great interest is being shown in fast reactors. Dr. Yiftah is the author of a standard work on fast reactors and the Israelis are showing considerable interest in the British work at Dounreay. Another project which is attracting some interest is the American Atomic Energy Commission's plan to co-operate with some firms in using water vapour from a heat reactor. Some people in Israel are arguing that this might be a method of desalination to help in providing the water requirements for Israel's ambitious plans to develop the Negev. On the whole, both this and fast reactors can be regarded only as possibilities which are being studied.

As far as delivery systems are concerned, Israel has not and cannot be expected to get a medium or heavy bomber. The doctrine of the air force is entirely subject to army thinking and is designed for army support, supply and paratrooping. The types in service are the British *Meteor* jet fighter, which is approaching retirement, the French *Mystère* and *Super Mystère* fighters, the French *Vautour* bomber, and the French *Noratlas* transport. The *Mirage 3* supersonic fighter will follow. There are no plans for modernizing the bomber force with anything beyond the *Vautour*, since supersonic bombing strikes can be done by the *Super Mystères* or *Mirage 3s*. The only French bomber which Israel could consider buying would be the *Mirage 4*, which will have unnecessarily long range and will be very expensive. It is most unlikely that Russia, Britain or the United States would sell a modern bomber to Israel for conventional purposes, let alone nuclear purposes. It seems, then, that the *Vautour* is the most important delivery system at present (though the fact that El Al's *Britannias* are committed to the air force and the possibilities of the *Noratlas* transports should not be overlooked). The *Vautours* would carry a 6,000—8,000 pound bomb in their bomb bay, a weight which Israeli designers and engineers would probably be able to meet if they embarked seriously on a nuclear bomb programme.

While it would obviously be beyond the resources of the country to build a high performance bomber, some sort of rocket weapon might be possible. A rocket establishment is now working inside the Ministry of Defence and has produced a two-stage solid fuel meteorological rocket which in 1961 carried a sodium flare up to 50 miles. This programme was pursued in secrecy and nothing is known of what might follow. The fuel appears to be successful and could presumably be adapted to a simple or complex bombardment weapon using elemental guidance, possibly under radio control. Since Israel's entire defence policy is directed against the territory of close neighbours, the small range requirement makes the guidance and propulsion problems comparatively simple. From these facts, and from the fact that the Ministry of Defence is sponsoring the development of the electronics industry, one can draw a variety of conclusions. There is at present no evidence available one way or the other beyond the fact that the expense of a rocket weapon does not now appear to be justified.

Almost all the political and military thought in Israel is opposed, at least publicly, to nuclear weapons. On a number of occasions, the Government has denied that it was producing an atomic bomb. On December 21st, 1960, for example, Dr. Shimshon Junitchman, a Herut member of the Knesset, asked the Prime Minister, Mr. Ben-Gurion, if he could give the source of the report that an atomic bomb was being produced in Israel. The Prime Minister replied: 'The report is either a deliberate or an unwitting untruth. The Government of Israel, as is well known, proposed general and total disarmament in Israel and the neighbouring Arab states, on condition that there would be a mutual right of inspection by Israel in the Arab states and by the Arab states in Israel. We proposed that this should be done even before the attainment of a universal agreement on general disarmament based on the principles of mutual inspection. The origin of this false report is evidently the atomic research being undertaken by our scientists in Israel'[1] While noting the denial here that anything was being done, it will also be seen that the Prime Minister said nothing of the future intentions of the Government and introduced the irrelevant issue of general disarmament in the area. If his remarks on this subject suggest anything about Israel's policy on nuclear weapons, they can be held to be saying the same thing about non-nuclear weapons; and it goes without saying that the country is doing everything it can to make itself as powerful in conventional weapons as possible.

Israeli defence policy is directed to survival in the face of Arab hostility. It is strongly defensive but it also contains a substantial element of deterrence. Indeed, it is possible to explain some of the ambiguities of statements on nuclear

[1] *Jerusalem Post*: December 22nd, 1960.

weapons by the desire to keep a certain uncertainty alive in the minds of the Arab Governments. Israelis look back with some satisfaction on the rumour among the Fedaheen during the Sinai campaign that they had nuclear weapons, and they like to encourage their reputation for genius and secrecy which leaves their enemies continuously uncertain about what they really have. Over even quite public things, such as the British *Centurion* tanks, they have deliberately maintained secrecy for a considerable time. By giving Arab intelligence a bad time over occasional things they believe that they can force them continuously to overrate Israel's power. This adds to the deterrent.

The great deterrent, however, is the army. This relies on high individual quality to compensate for inferiority in certain equipment and on reserves to match the large regular forces of Egypt and Iraq. Defence spending, though secret, is probably less than 10 per cent of the gross national product and so is less relatively than that of the United States and comparable with that of Britain. On the whole, it is regrettably high for a country which is urgently concerned with forming capital; but in view of Israel's great capacity for raising money abroad it cannot be considered an intolerable burden. Israeli defence planners must obviously have wondered if a stock of nuclear weapons would ease this defence burden. They are superficially attractive as an alternative or supplement to the deterrent provided by the army. Would not the threat of nuclear attacks on Cairo, Baghdad and Damascus frighten the Arabs out of the war of obliteration as effectively as the Israeli Army? The notion has its appeal, especially since the essential element of deterrence, credibility, would be present in the Israeli case to a greater extent than perhaps any other country in the world. The Arabs believe that the Israelis are determined and ruthless people who will stop at nothing to survive: what would make nuclear weapons more credible than this?

Closer examination makes this view less tenable. A country which has difficulty in persuading anyone to sell it a medium tank and cannot obtain a surface to air guided weapon is not likely to be sold nuclear weapons or delivery systems in any but the most extreme circumstances. The policy of the Russians towards Egypt, however, in the event that Israel produced nuclear weapons, might prove disastrous from the Israeli point of view. It is generally felt in Israeli government circles that in these circumstances the Russians would make nuclear bombs available in some way to the Egyptians. If that happened, the Israelis would be at a grave disadvantage both in numbers and sophistication. Worse, they would be hard pressed to maintain a position from which they could retaliate effectively since their territory is so small and narrow. Warning time would be negligible and, if the Russians made any number of weapons available, the Egyptians might be tempted to make the war of obliteration a massive nuclear strike. Serious thought has been given to these possibilities in Israel and leading men in government insist that Israel's military interest is, and must continue to be, to keep nuclear weapons out of the Middle East.

The extent to which nuclear weapons would fulfil the deterrent role of the army is also doubtful. The opportunities open to Israel's enemies for minor attacks and raids of every kind across the long desert frontiers have been exploited for years and have been met with both defensive and retaliatory actions (of which the Sinai campaign of 1956 is the leading case). Nuclear retaliation would not be credible or sane for these purposes. The army is also used as a deterrent for certain things which do not directly involve a breach of Israel's frontiers: a union of Jordan and Egypt based on the over-throw of King Hussein; the remilitarisation of the Gulf of Eliath by the Egyptians and an attempt to reimpose the blockade on Israeli shipping to the East; or an attack on Israel's merchant fleet on the high seas. In spite of the credibility which might be attached to an Israeli nuclear force if the country was in danger of destruction, it could obviously not be used to deter such secondary actions. The army would have to maintain superiority for these purposes. Thus the logic which has led the western powers to add conventional deterrence to their nuclear deterrence can be seen well in advance by Israeli military planners. Nuclear weapons would not ease the defence burden.

Two other serious possibilities must be examined. Can the Israelis be sure that they will retain conventional dominance indefinitely? And what will they do if one or more of the Arab countries contrives to obtain nuclear weapons? To the first of these questions, the official answer is 'yes' for the foreseeable future: the best Russian equipment is not expected to tilt the balance. Studies have been done of the potential of the Arab countries on pessimistic assumptions and they have shown that the rise of population and increase of wealth which can be anticipated in Israel will compensate for any Arab improvements for at least 15 years. The Israelis must, of course, make the assumption that they will be able to buy sophisticated arms from one country or another; but there seems little reason to doubt this as long as the Russians are supplying the main Arab countries. The western powers are committed to the survival of Israel, though they prefer the arms sales which are the military evidence for this to be done by those NATO countries, such as France and Canada, which have the least to lose with other Middle Eastern powers. The future of the Israel-Arab balance of power is also dependent on political developments and above all on progress towards unity in the Arab world. Israel has come to rely on Arab particularism, especially in Jordan, and there are always those who argue that the day of Arab unity cannot be far distant. But the years of failure are dragging on and the break-up of the United Arab Republic suggests that the urge to effective unity is weaker than ever before. Events do not therefore seem to be running militarily against Israel. If a powerful Arab leader rises up and obtains the serious support of a great power in developing a fighting force capable of overwhelming Israel, nuclear weapons might well emerge as a final deterrent. The evidence that the Israeli Government is working towards an option to produce these weapons at some future date if it should think them necessary can probably be traced to this possibility. If this is correct, they are being held in reserve for a development which at present appears unlikely.

What about the possibility that one of the Arab countries will get nuclear weapons? No-one in Israel believes that Egypt or Iraq will produce them for themselves for a long time to come, if ever, and presumably such a programme would be automatically matched and exceeded by Israel itself. The important uncertainty is Russian intentions. If the Soviet Union were to give nuclear weapons to the Egyptians, the Israeli armed forces would obviously be incapable of maintaining parity on their own: the country would have to rely on an equally sophisticated nuclear power. So, like the Indian Government, Israelis put their faith in the Americans to maintain a local deterrent in such circumstances. The presumption is that a local arming of an associated power with such weapons would draw the east-west conflict into the area concerned. This seems so obvious that the Russians are not expected to give the idea serious consideration. Nevertheless, the Israelis constantly seek American assurances which are given from time to time in a general way.

Opinion about the morality of atomic weapons in Israel is very much divided. On the one hand, almost everyone believes in a vigorous military policy; on the other, there is a strong Socialist tradition which spreads across the ruling centre and which goes back to the radical roots of all the main political parties except the right-wing Herut. Old ideals are sacred in Israel where force, as understood in the Haganah and the great war of independence, has become merged with the great radical pioneer tradition. In this there is no experience of mass bombing. Many thinking people can be found who are anxious that their country should have nothing to do with these things. It may be doubted, however, whether this climate of opinion would influence the Israeli Government if it considered it militarily and economically desirable to equip itself with nuclear weapons. Since the important decisions at an early stage would be taken one by one and could be justified by the requirements of a power programme and a conventional delivery system, it would be difficult for opposition to crystallize until a late stage. The French experience illustrates this. Many people in Israel believe that the Government is pursuing just such a programme at present and it is possible to find much suspicion of the defence authorities. Nevertheless, no opposition can be mounted at present, since there is officially no nuclear weapons programme. Forecasting the drift of political opinion if the official centre decided that nuclear weapons were desirable would be very difficult. On the whole, the most important party, Mapai, and the more left-wing Achdut Avodah would probably find that their Socialist principles would not stand in the way of something which appeared essential to Israel's security. The Communists, of course, would not take this line: nor would the left-wing socialist party Mapam.

With China, Sweden, Switzerland, and West Germany, then, Israel must be regarded as an uncertain country for the future. Like China, Israel seems to derive certain benefits from the reputation for being on the way towards the bomb. This spreads respect and prestige and the sort of denials which have come out of Ottawa and New Delhi cannot be expected from Peking or Tel Aviv. But like the West Germans, they can see the perils which would open for them if the Russians became convinced that this is what they were doing. Politically, the policy seems to be to keep Cairo wondering while giving mild reassurances to the great powers. Militarily, it is almost certain to watch every possibility and plan for conventional fighting while studying a nuclear strategy. And scientifically, it is to build a strong base in research and widen the needed technology wherever this can be done without a heavy and unprofitable investment. An Israeli bomb can be ruled out for many years; but it can probably never be ruled out absolutely.

PART III

The Spread

Chapter 12

The Present Position

ONE of the important conclusions of this study is that the spread of nuclear weapons is by no means inevitable. Though many countries are technically equipped for the manufacture of nuclear weapons, comparatively few have chosen to do so. Indeed only China (and she very ambiguously) has indicated that she will obtain nuclear power independently. It is not yet certain that any other nation will decide to follow suit. Nations do not decide to manufacture weapons merely because they realise it is feasible; and the spread of nuclear weapons is obviously not as inexorable even as the spread of the juke-box.

It is also clear that the motives which determine national policies on nuclear weapons are varied, and that they are compounded on different recipes. In Canada, for example, a domestic nuclear policy is frankly deplored. In India a similar feeling is universally expressed though it may be tempered by a greater awareness of military insecurity. In Sweden a fear of compromising the special and delicate relationship between Finland and the Soviet Union plays an important part in discussions of nuclear defence. Israel appears to be held back from nuclear policies by an unwillingness to see the Middle East infested with nuclear weapons. In Switzerland great weight is given to the thesis that nuclear weapons might help to ensure neutrality. All this implies that there can be no simple rule separating the potential nuclear powers from those which are likely to set their faces against nuclear policies, either now or in the future.

A further conclusion is that nations may take steps to provide a military nuclear capacity without finally deciding to manufacture weapons for themselves. This is most clearly exemplified by the technological plans which have been laid in India. The effect of these will be to make it possible for a decision to manufacture weapons to be implemented more quickly than would be possible without planning in advance. So far there is no suggestion that the government of India intends to exercise this option and the steps which have been taken are consistent with the development of peaceful nuclear power. Because of the similarity of many peaceful and military developments in nuclear technology, it must always be difficult to tell which nations are trying to provide themselves with an option on nuclear manufacture.

Both India and Sweden may be in a position by 1963 or 1964 to embark on their own nuclear weapons, and could hope to explode their first weapons within five years of taking the decision. Though the course of development in Israel is more obscure, she may be seeking to attain a similar option about 1970. To these nations the option to produce nuclear weapons offers political flexibility in an unpredictable world. In present circumstances, none of these three countries appears willing to take up an option to manufacture weapons even if it had it. In all of them the political disadvantages of such a course, though varied, are thought to be overwhelming.

Germany is a more difficult and complicated case. For one thing, there can be no doubt of the nation's technical capacity for making bombs. There is the growing demand for reassurance that nuclear weapons, strategic as well as tactical, will be used in the nation's defence, and it is by no means clear whether and how this demand will be met. Continued dissatisfaction with the credibility of the nuclear defence of Germany could persuade some future German government to manufacture nuclear weapons for itself in spite of the difficulty of deploying these safely and effectively in the Federal Republic, let alone testing them.

The studies in Part II do not exhaust the list of nations technically capable of making nuclear weapons, either soon or at some time in the future. A fuller list was produced some time ago by the National Planning Association in the United States.[1] The most commonly quoted part of that document is a classification of nations according to their technical ability to embark on the production of nuclear weapons. The report

[1] *The Nth Country Problem and Arms Control*, National Planning Association, January 1960.

concluded that in the 'near future' decisions to make these
weapons could be taken by Belgium, Canada, China, Czechoslovakia, France, East Germany, West Germany, India, Italy,
Japan, Sweden and Switzerland. In a second category of
nations economically strong but equipped with only limited
scientific manpower were Australia, Austria, Denmark, Finland, Hungary, the Netherlands, Poland, and Yugoslavia.
Finally there was a category of nations provided with some of
the sources of military nuclear power but limited economically
and in terms of skilled manpower. This included Argentina,
Brazil, Mexico, Norway Spain and South Africa. One of the
results of the publication of this classification has been the
frequent repetition of statements that a 'dozen' countries were
on the threshold of military nuclear power, and that as many
again might become nuclear powers in the foreseeable future.
These inferences from the NPA report have been widely made
in spite of careful qualifications elsewhere in the document.
Such a classification can only be a partial guide to an assessment of which nations are about to become nuclear powers.
This study has been concerned to show the technical, economic,
military and political factors which also bear on the choices of
governments; but even on technical grounds alone it is possible to disagree with the NPA document on the grounds that
it does not take sufficient account of special factors which
might hinder or help individual nations from making nuclear
weapons.

Though such countries as Belgium and Italy are so technically advanced that they could take an immediate and realistic decision to manufacture nuclear weapons and could expect
to implement this within seven or eight years there is no prospect that they will take this step. Both of them have, for
instance, agreed that fuel for atomic power stations shall be
supplied under the most rigorous safeguards that this cannot
be used for military purposes. In neither of them is this seen as
an infringement of national sovereignty. The same is true of
Japan, which might be technically capable of manufacturing
weapons for itself. In practice that nation has almost osten-
tatiously sought to obtain nuclear supplies under strict control
from international bodies such as the IAEA (though there

were parliamentary misgivings when it was necessary to agree to the terms of control and inspection attached to the supply of British fuel for a nuclear reactor soon to be commissioned north of Tokyo). Czechoslovakia and East Germany have advanced programmes for the peaceful use of atomic power but there is no reason to assume that this will lead to the independent possession of nuclear weapons. This question is part of the total relationship of these countries to the Soviet Union: and if, as is widely believed in the West, they are under the secure control of Moscow, the apparent possession of nuclear weapons by their governments and armed forces would not, in principle, involve the spread of weapons. It seems reasonable to assume that Russians will only share where they know they can control. More remotely there are nations such as Yugoslavia and Brazil whose technical capabilities are not yet sufficient to permit a decision to manufacture weapons, but which may be in a position to embark on a military programme within this decade. For different reasons these nations may be expected to follow India in taking out an option on the manufacture of weapons. There is however no likelihood that this could be exercised before 1975. These conclusions about the capacity of nations to make weapons for themselves are summarised in the accompanying table.

It has become increasingly obvious in the course of this study that there are a growing number of political mechanisms which serve at present to keep the spread of nuclear weapons in check. The policies of the great powers are and will continue to be the most important influence. In the West, as has been seen, the determination of the United States to prevent the emergence of nuclear powers has been codified in legislation regulating the sharing of materials and technology concerning nuclear weapons. This was put into formal international policy through its 1961 disarmament proposals to the United Nations which suggested (for a first stage) that:

States owning nuclear weapons would not relinquish control of such weapons to any nation not owning them and would not transmit to any such nation information or material necessary for their manufacture. States not owning nuclear

	Option on a Bomb	Mood in 1962	General Position
United States	1945	Nuclear	Strategic and tactical force
Soviet Union	1949	Nuclear	Strategic and tactical force
Britain	1952	Nuclear	Strategic force
Canada	1957	Non-nuclear	Hostile to national force
France	1960	Nuclear	Creating force
India	1963–5	Non-nuclear	As Canada, but creating option
China	1963–5?	Nuclear	Unclear
Germany	1965	Nuclear	Seeking allied arrangement
Italy	1966	Non-nuclear	Allied arrangements only
Japan	1966	Non-nuclear	Hostile to nuclear weapons
Sweden	1969	Non-nuclear	As Canada, but in dispute
Israel	1968–71	Non-nuclear	Creating option
Switzerland	1970	Non-nuclear	As Sweden
Australia	1971	Non-nuclear	Uncertain

Note: Countries in bold type are the ones studied in Part II.

weapons would not manufacture them or attempt to obtain control of such weapons belonging to other states.[1]

The Soviet Government has taken an equally clear line. In its October, 1961, memorandum to the United Nations, it said:

In the Soviet Government's opinion, there is a possibility at present for concluding an agreement under which nuclear powers would pledge themselves not to pass nuclear weapons to other countries, while states not possessing nuclear weapons would undertake not to manufacture these weapons or buy them from other powers. Obviously, there is no need to emphasise what an acute danger to peace can be created by the expansion of the circle of powers possessing nuclear weapons or the secret of their manufacture, irrespective of whether it would be an 'individual' possession or the passing of such weapons within the framework of one or other military bloc system.[2]

Among the other nuclear powers, Britain adopts the same policies as the United States. The attitude of France is less clear. As a result of the initiative of Ireland, the United Nations General Assembly has, however, committed itself on this subject. On November 20th, 1959, it recognised by 68–0 (France and the Soviet bloc abstaining) that 'the danger now exists that an increase in the number of states possessing nuclear weapons may occur, aggravating international tension and the difficulty of maintaining world peace, and thus rendering more difficult the attainment of a general disarmament agreement.'[3] On December 20th, 1960, by the same vote (though this time the U.S., Britain, France, Australia and 22 other non-Communist states abstained), the General Assembly:

1. Calls upon all Governments to make every effort to achieve permanent agreement on the prevention of the wider dissemination of such [nuclear] weapons:

[1] U.S. Proposals, September 26th, 1961
[2] *Soviet News*, London, October 6th, 1961.
[3] Department of State Publication 7008, Vol. 2. p. 1547.

2. Calls upon Powers producing such weapons, as a temporary and voluntary measure pending the negotiation of such a permanent agreement, to refrain from relinquishing control of such weapons to any nation not posessing them and from transmitting to it the information necessary for their manufacture:

3. Calls upon powers not possessing such weapons, on a similar temporary and voluntary basis, to refrain from manufacturing these weapons and from otherwise attempting to acquire them.[1]

The influence of the great powers on the policies of smaller nations is also expressed in the degree of security from attack which is conferred by their alliance. This is exemplified by the anxieties in West Germany over the decline—real or imagined—in the credibility of the American deterrent as a means of ensuring the integrity of the Federal Republic. It is not surprising that changes in the balance of international security should be accompanied by changes in the attitudes of non-nuclear powers towards the desirability of nuclear weapons. By their policies in maintaining the credibility of their nuclear forces as defences for their allies, the nuclear powers will inevitably exercise an important influence on the spread of independent nuclear power.

On the purely technical side there can be no doubt that the progress of time will lessen the difficulties which at present would confront non-nuclear powers embarking on the manufacture of nuclear explosives. The steady growth of the peaceful applications of nuclear power must increase the ease with which nations will be able to recruit the skilled men needed to mount a military programme. The same developments are also likely to simplify the manufacture of nuclear explosives, and reduce the cost of stockpiling warheads. On the other hand there is no foreseeable likelihood that innovations like the gas centrifuge machine for separating fissile uranium from the natural material will radically simplify the process of making nuclear explosives. As for the means of delivery, they appear to

---

[1] Department of State Publication 7172, page 373. A similar resolution was passed on December 4th, 1961.

be maintaining a high rate of innovation because of the endless interaction of offence and defence. Here there is no sign of slackening, though in the most advanced countries delivery systems are becoming cheaper with the arrival of solid fuel missiles. In the absence of sharing, however, there is no real possibility that middle powers will be seriously affected by these economies because the cost of development remains so high. Taken all in all, it may be expected that the price of a serious nuclear weapons force will go on rising while that of a blackmail force with an inferior or improvised delivery system will decline a little. It should be recognised, however, that the increase in cost may be matched by the rising wealth and industrial strength of a number of countries. It is this which will make possible the steady increase in the number of nuclear powers.

That increase, however, will only take place if there are convincing arguments among the new industrial nations for obtaining nuclear weapons. It may be expected that the kind of arguments which have been put forward successfully in the British and French cases and are being argued in some of the other countries studied will recur over the years. So will the objections which experience has taught. On the whole there are seven groups of arguments to be found in favour of nuclear weapons. They are:

1. That they are the only deterrent against an enemy who is himself armed with atomic weapons.

2. That they are desirable replacements for conventional forces because they are more effective.

3. That they provide a cheaper defence and that the sort of technologies involved in creating a nuclear weapons force are useful to an advanced economy.

4. That they are an ultimate guarantee and embodiment of independence.

5. That they are a valuable source of prestige with allies and with the world in general.

6. That they are a useful guarantee against the possibility that a great power guarantor will lose his nerve in a crisis.

7. That they enable a country to take a more useful part in disarmament negotiations.

The most obvious attribute of atomic weapons is their great explosive power. This is sometimes imprudently forgotten. Military staffs everywhere recognise that bombs with the explosive power of those dropped on the Japanese cities in 1945 are now deployed in tactical military roles; yet even one of these may have an explosive power equal to the total weight of the conventional explosives carried by a thousand heavily laden road vehicles. The warheads of the ballistic missiles now in service are more powerful still: that of such a comparatively small missile as the *Minuteman* is equivalent in explosive power to a decade's normal output of conventional explosives from the British or German chemical industry.

In most countries, there is evidence that those branches of the armed forces which would gain the most decisive advantage in their operational roles are most active in promoting a decision in favour of producing bombs. In the early post-war period, the only use for them which was seriously contemplated was strategic bombing. This was strongly taken up in Britain, where Royal Air Force Bomber Command had a strongly-held strategic bombing doctrine. Indeed without the new weapons, the R.A.F. would undoubtedly have had to give up strategic bombing which could not now be effective with conventional weapons against so distant a target as the Soviet Union. Defences have progressed too far in relation to the offence. It is important, however, that strategic bombing does not figure in the thinking of most of the countries which we are now considering. The Royal Canadian Air Force is defensively minded and those countries (such as Sweden, India and Israel) which maintain bomber forces do so as a force for support of the army or navy. This is not to say that the attractions of becoming a strategic bombing power may not appeal to new countries; it is merely that it would in most cases be a new role and is therefore one for which strong support does not already exist in the armed forces.

Tactically, nuclear weapons are militarily attractive for several purposes. The most important of these is probably interdiction bombing—the destruction of an enemy's supply lines—in a situation in which forces are operating relatively far from their base. This includes the bombing of ports as well as supply lines. Armies also believe that the simple possession of such weapons will deny an enemy army the advantages of concentration, since a concentrated target could be effectively attacked. Tactical theories based on the use of atomic power have been widely considered over the past ten years and have gained an important place in the tactical doctrine of the United States Army. In those countries where military staffs have considerable influence, these considerations must be expected to carry weight. This is in fact the case with Switzerland which is as serious about the matter as any country outside China. It is also true of Sweden and also, perhaps, Germany and Israel, though in these two cases the political problems are so obvious that they influence even the mood of the soldiers.

Recently there has been strong evidence that a long-term study of nuclear tactics has led the United States armed forces to a certain disillusion with tactical nuclear warfare. A similar conclusion is evident in Britain in a recent article by Sir Solly Zuckerman, the Chief Scientist of the Ministry of Defence.[1] There is no sign at present that this change has had an effect in such countries as Sweden, Germany and Switzerland; but it may over the next few years—and would reduce the military pressure for a bomb programme.

In other categories such as air defence and naval warfare there are good reasons for using nuclear weapons. In general, however, these uses are so secondary that the staffs concerned have not pressed strongly for their adoption. As the subject has arisen mainly in the circumstances of the North Atlantic alliance and the air defence of North America, it has been settled with the usual provisions concerning United States control over warheads.

Nevertheless, the fact that nuclear weapons have changed the character of warfare itself is obvious to all nations. Atomic weapons have, for example, made certain types of weapons practicable which would not have developed in the days of conventional explosives. This difference could make a non-nuclear status appear increasingly archaic. It also raises the question of the morale of fighting services. It is felt in a number of countries that the welfare of their armies depends on the

[1] *Foreign Affairs*, January, 1962.

knowledge that their equipment is technically as good as that of an opposing or even an allied army.

These military considerations appear now to be much more important than economic ones. Nevertheless, as economies develop, troops become more expensive and fewer men—especially the technicians able to man modern conventional weapons—can be kept under arms. The cost of large conventional armies rises steeply. Nuclear weapons can offer important savings in manpower and can even make it possible to offer a defence in areas where a conventional defence could not hope to be effective. For example, for NATO to defend Western Europe with conventional weapons would probably need several times its present force targets. Russia's reduction of its forces by one-third in 1960 was justified by the increase in the fire power of modern weapons (though there have now been second thoughts). Without going into the difficult and unproved military argument about whether nuclear weapons on both sides make more or less troops necessary, the country which is finding its military burdens too heavy is going to find atomic bombs an obvious attraction. Small nations subject to this temptation will find, however, that they must make a fixed investment to produce nuclear weapons which will take some time to yield the dividends in cheapness which they are seeking. Such countries are not usually capable of creating whole new industries for purely military purposes: they buy their modern and sophisticated equipment from one of the great powers. Indeed, the countries which may have the greatest economic need of atomic firepower may be precisely those to whom its attainment entails the greatest economic difficulty.

This economic argument played a most important part in British military thought from the earliest post-war days and is still behind the anxiety of the British government that NATO should not dilute its nuclear defence of Europe. Even the 1957 British reductions in her forces in Germany were justified by the argument that equivalent firepower was being provided by the introduction of nuclear weapons. The French Government, by contrast, has not been tempted by this reasoning. It has seen its *force de frappe* as an addition and not a substitute for its conventional armed forces. In the climate of the 1960s, it seems most unlikely that general staffs will argue that they can get along with fewer conventional troops if they are provided with atomic weapons. It is now obvious that there are so many situations in which they cannot be used that a reduction in manpower and expense equal to that required for the nuclear weapons force would in many cases be difficult to achieve. Over-all economies would be rare.

The hope that the creation of a nuclear force would stimulate commerce has occasionally been expressed. In Britain, it has been argued that the pursuit of a comprehensive military nuclear power programme would help create self-sufficiency in power and help advanced industries such as the aircraft industry and the electronics industry. While it has undoubtedly done all these things, the industries in question have used a high proportion of the country's talent and have not, on the whole, brought in export earnings commensurate with the money spent on them. As time has gone on, the delivery systems needed for a modern nuclear weapons force—particularly rocket weapons—have become more and more divorced from any civil applications. Since smaller powers are not nuclear powers, weapons tailored for nuclear delivery have not had an export market—something which a country like Britain or France normally expects to find for the product of a major development programme. Certainly it can be said that this sort of argument played little or no part in the French decision and cannot now be found elsewhere.

Great though the military or the economic advantages of atomic power may seem, this is always likely to be subordinate to its political advantages. For the coming of atomic power has done more than make possible radically new forms of warfare; it has also suggested novel kinds of international policies. Though it may be argued that the motives which cause nations to seek influence on the course of world affairs have not changed for centuries, the means by which they can do so have changed almost out of recognition. The particular features of atomic warfare which have most directly influenced the formulation of international policies are its potential destructiveness, its speed, and the likelihood that strategic nuclear attack with modern delivery systems cannot be warded off. Nuclear

attack has been described as 'annihilating', and though this
may be something of an exaggeration, there is no doubt that it
could set back a nation many generations in its economic and
cultural development. The price of nuclear warfare might not
be extinction in the ecological sense, but it might easily
amount to the annulment of several centuries of human en-
deavour. This is a novelty in international relations.

An immediate consequence of this has been the emphasis
given to the concept of deterrence in policy-making. Though
nations have traditionally used the threat of conventional
warfare, backed up by powerful military forces, as a means of
safeguarding national interests, this is radically different from
the use of threats of nuclear warfare as retaliation for mis-
demeanours of a military or a diplomatic character. There is
every reason to expect that other countries besides the present
atomic powers are attracted by the foreign policies which
nuclear deterrence or even threats make possible. Effectiveness must be limited by the prospect that the force could
never hope to be large by world standards, but it could be
important regionally in the absence of great power guarantees. There is the familiar French argument that a small
nation can deter adequately with a small force because this
need be matched only to the nation's value as an objective, not
the strength of those which threaten it. As it happens, most
countries seem to expect that a nuclear force would in fact
produce a great power guarantee of their regional rival. The
Israeli Government appears to accept the possibility that an
Israeli bomb might lead to the nuclear armament of Egypt and
the same appears to be true as between India and Pakistan.
The situation in South America or Africa is less clear. Brazilian
or South African nuclear weapons might well lead to pressure
for nuclear guarantees from neighbouring states, but the
situation is too intimately tied up with the political climate of
the day to be predictable.

Prestige in the broadest sense was an important factor in
both the British and French decisions and is presumably predominant in Chinese thought. When it comes to those who see
themselves as middle powers, however, this may have a different character. Since nuclear weapons will no longer be confined

to great powers, they will no longer be a sign of a great power. Something is no longer a symbol of opulence or greatness if it is possessed by those who are by common consent neither opulent nor great. On the other hand, if those one regards as equals obtain it, the desire not to fall behind may become strong. In particular, a change of heart in Canada might do something to restore the mood of inevitability to the question of the spread of nuclear weapons. A Swiss or Swedish bomb programme would in some sense make Germany's present status less tolerable; and the spread of nuclear weapons to the Communist countries of eastern Europe—even if this was in fact controlled politically from Moscow—might also have an important psychological effect on the Federal Republic. A Chinese bomb, especially if wielded belligerently, is bound to have far-reaching effects on India and Japan and even Australia. Sure signs that Israel is taking a firm option on nuclear weapons might have a serious influence on a number of countries.

The key issue here is the prestige which the next decade will attach to these weapons. There can be no doubt that the prestige of the military atom fell heavily in the 1957-62 period with the confusion of French policy, the depression of the British over *Blue Streak*, and the switch of American emphasis from nuclear to conventional forces. A growth in the non-nuclear club from its present slim membership of Canada, India and perhaps Germany will tend even more to reduce the prestige benefits of a weapons programme. When an American air force officer went through the sound barrier in 1947, it was rightly regarded as a spectacular and historic achievement. Yet in 1960 even an exceptionally fine interceptor like the *Draken*, able to do a wide variety of military jobs at twice the speed of sound, brings little prestige to Sweden, with only one twenty-fifth the population of the United States. An Italian in orbit in 1980 will presumably impress few people outside Italy. Prestige weapons are rare weapons. We may thus conclude that nuclear weapons are unlikely to spread around the world as an obvious way of obtaining prestige. This factor will only exercise an influence if they become so common that it is a mark of inferiority not to have them. That day is distant except among those, such as China, who aspire to great power status.

Whether Germany, Japan and India will share these emotions remains to be seen.

As the pressure from prestige considerations eases, uncertainty about alliances may weigh in the other direction. Much of the debate over nuclear weapons in NATO (and among countries like India and Sweden which in fact depend on the United States) is a debate about the United States nuclear weapons force, both strategic and tactical. When will it be used? Can they rely on it to defend them? Can they increase their control over it? Can they place themselves in a position from which it will be possible to ensure that it is used? These are the question which eventually get asked and for which no clear answers have emerged. From the point of view, strictly, of the spread of weapons to new powers, there is no doubt that a nuclear America, ready and willing to resort to a nuclear strategy for its allies, is a strong discouragement to national forces. Some might, of course, think the remedy worse than the disease. Nevertheless, the fact remains that the celebrated remark of Mr. Herter that he could not conceive of a decision for all-out nuclear war 'unless the facts showed clearly we are in danger of all-out devastation ourselves',[1] President Kennedy's statement that 'our objective now is to increase our ability to confine our response to non-nuclear weapons',[2] and the new doctrines of men like Dr. Kissinger, have combined to give the impression that the American nuclear umbrella may be limited. This issue was discussed at length in Chapter 6. Although it is most prominent in relation to Germany, it may be important over a period of years for a number of countries —and deserves the serious consideration it is getting in the formation of U.S. policy.

One of the most remarkable commentaries on the state of political debate, as it is today, is the prevalence of the argument that it is necessary for particular states to develop nuclear weapons in order to increase their say in disarmament negotiations. This is frequently heard in Great Britain and France (which have, indeed, a notable record in pioneering disarmament thought, though this preceded the French bomb) and is

[1] April 21st, 1959,
[2] Message to Congress on Defence Budget, March 28th 1961.
S.N.W.—O*

at times mentioned in Sweden and elsewhere. Canada, by contrast, is definitely influenced in her approach to nuclear weapons—particularly the live question of accepting American-controlled warheads—by her disarmament policy. This is a strong and important influence on government thought. Canada's feeling that her influence is increased through being non-nuclear is partly derived, perhaps, from the recognition by the powers after 1946 that she did in fact have the option and her inclusion in the Security Council negotiations which accompanied the Baruch Plan and later disarmament proposals. This argument could easily be eliminated for other countries if the powers took the sensible step in disarmament negotiations of treating those (such as Canada, India and Germany) who can build nuclear weapons as if they had done so.

On the general question of reputation, there is also the possibility that the possession of atomic weapons could damage a nation's position, both internationally and at home. The harm which could be done to a reputation obviously depends on what kind of reputation the country already has. This is not surprising; even in ordinary society some are more vulnerable than others. Habitual drunkenness has little effect on the reputation of convicted felons but may irreparably damage a politician or a religious leader. It seems that China would evoke few protests when its first atomic weapon is tested, but India would have to examine the extent to which its pacific intentions would be questioned. Several nations which have acquired a reputation for peacemaking fear that this would be lost by the manufacture of nuclear weapons. Tests can be particularly damaging. France lost some goodwill among the newly independent nations of West Africa as a result of its atomic tests in the Sahara; and American and British tests in the Pacific (especially those at Bikini in 1954) aroused opposition in Japan and elsewhere. The Soviet Union, though more immune to this type of criticism, exposed itself to a major western propaganda campaign by its tests of very large weapons in 1961. In general, as long as nuclear weapons are confined to the major powers, the evidence is that the general issue of prestige will weigh against acquiring them among most middle powers.

Chapter 13
The Future

WHAT are the dangers for the world if nuclear weapons
do spread steadily to new countries? It is widely
assumed that any further spread would be a threat to world
peace and a disastrous complication either in balancing terror
or enforcing disarmament—the two favourite prescriptions for
peace. Though there is much in this, if only because of the
uncertainties involved, it has suffered from overstatement. The
approach to this problem associated with Sir Charles Snow,
for example, has gone so far that the certainty of a great
atomic war is already asserted. This depends on a relation of
the chance of accident (spread day by day over the years) with
an assumption that the accidental use of one or two nuclear
weapons would automatically result in a massive nuclear
exchange. Since the chance increases with every new power,
the period during which the chance becomes a certainty
presumably decreases. Sir Charles Snow has written[1]: 'Within
at the most ten years some of those bombs are going off. That
is a certainty.' Bertrand Russell has concluded from this that
'if C. P. Snow is right—and there is no reason whatever to
think him wrong—at some day during the next ten years . . .
a very large proportion of our population will be killed outright, and the remainder will die a slow and agonizing death.'[2]
This is an extreme statement of the general belief that the more
there are of these things and the more owners they have the
more likely they are to be used.

This doctrine is obviously in conflict with the notion that
nuclear weapons are a unique deterrent. Taken to its logical
conclusion, it can be used to demonstrate that the greater the
spread of nuclear weapons the smaller the chance of war. The

[1] *The Moral Un-neutrality of Science*, Monthly Review, February,
1961, p. 156.
[2] *Has Man a Future?*, George Allen & Unwin, p. 108.

nuclear shadows which impose caution on Russians in Berlin or American reconnaissance aircraft would extend to the dozen minor conflicts between non-nuclear powers. This is the essence of the argument; and it was elaborately expounded in France when the debate on the *force de frappe* was at its height. In its pure form, it is now seldom expressed—though it might be expected to re-emerge with the theorists of any country embarking on nuclear weapons against domestic or world opinion. As with the statistical argument, it contains an element of truth. No doubt conventional conflicts between East and West in Europe would have been more likely in the last 15 years if it had not been for the awesome dominance of nuclear weapons over any use of force. These weapons provided the main incentive to keep the Korean War severely limited. The wary tread of the great powers in the last decade is likely to be a permanent feature of relations between nuclear powers.

The implications of this can, however, be no more than a consolation if nuclear weapons spread widely. Where none of the political conflicts between Russia and the United States are matters of life and death, those between Israel and her Arab neighbours, Pakistan and India, South Africa and black Africa, or Yugoslavia and her Communist neighbours might appear to some of these governments as an issue for which anything must be risked. The threat of mass destruction can be a great controller of tempers in tense situations. But there are likely to be tempers which even this threat cannot control; and, if this happens, the resulting conflict will take on a horror which was only suggested by the sufferings of Hiroshima and Nagasaki. The real danger is the use of nuclear weapons in such conflicts. Where a country (such as Canada or Sweden) seems unlikely to find itself in this position, a nuclear weapons programme is undesirable primarily for the example it sets.

Apart from this direct danger of turning local wars into nuclear wars, there are a number of other reasons why the spread of these weapons cannot be expected to serve the cause of peace and stability. Broadly, there are five serious aspects to this: (1) the instability of the period during which particular

countries are known to be developing weapons but have not;
(2) the inevitability of imbalance as between rivals as the
spread goes on; (3) the possibility that as nuclear forces grow
surprise attack may become safe for one side or another; (4)
the danger that small powers may obtain the ability to draw
great powers into nuclear wars (the notion of catalytic war);
(5) the complication of disarmament or arms control negotiations; (6) the general increase in tension which is likely to
accompany an increase in the world-wide levels of military
power.

The first of these, the gestation period, applies to those
countries which do not have a firm guarantee from a major
power or who could not be certain that this guarantee would
survive if they were building weapons. As long as secrecy is
impossible during, at the least, the last two or three years
before an operational force exists, a country like Israel or the
Federal Republic of Germany might generate an urgent
atmosphere among its rivals. To this extent, a conventional
preventive war might become likely more because the simple
symmetry of nuclear weapons all round on which the familiar
French thesis rests would not be present. Much the same considerations—though now threatening nuclear conflict—apply
to the second and third categories of danger. In the second, a
country with a good lead might feel obliged to exploit it
before the enemy's ability to retaliate became so great as to be
unacceptable; in the third, there are likely to be periods in
which military planners can see a virtually certain capacity
to destroy an enemy's ability to retaliate by a sudden strike.
Where countries are very close to one another, tactical warning of air attack becomes negligible and the problem of mounting
a counter-force strike is greatly simplified.

While these three dangers seem to apply mainly to possible
local conflicts, the issue of catalytic war is more relevant to the
alliances. It is generally held that once a war is nuclear the
main limitation on it is removed. The ability to trigger a large
force becomes a powerful deterrent in the hands of a middle
power. Both the British and French nuclear forces have been
defended on the ground that they ensure an American nuclear
strategy in the defence of Europe. Though this notion has been

seriously questioned,[1] it is true enough to inject a new element of uncertainty into the strategic balance between the great powers. The desire to have control over a force large enough to make sure that a country's defence will in fact be nuclear is, as has been shown, a major element in the present official military thinking of Germany. Another aspect of catalytic war has been advanced by some American theorists who have argued that with a wide spread of nuclear weapons unidentifiable attacks might be launched. These might be intended to bring the great powers into a war of mutual destruction while leaving the source of the attacks in a powerful third position. The most skilled creators of war games might have difficulty in showing that a second rate power could get away with such a strike undetected, that the great powers would inevitably respond with massive retaliation on one another, that the third power would not suffer in this process, and that it would end up better off than it was before.[2] Nevertheless, the opportunities for blackmail, especially by a national leader known for his ruthlessness and irresponsibility, are obvious; and there can be little doubt that the spread of nuclear weapons to many states will make these weapons a more immediate fact in the life and policies of many nations.

As for disarmament and arms control, the difficulties of agreement among the nuclear powers might well be increased by larger numbers. While it is true that in many negotiations pressure to agree is put on the major powers by smaller powers, the chances that one or more new nuclear powers might be unwilling to accept a control system or to give up weapons are quite strong. Just as France was unwilling to accept a moratorium on tests during the 1958–61 great power moratorium and would not have conformed to a test ban had it been agreed, it may be expected that any country embarking on nuclear weapons will resist agreements of this kind. Once the bombs have beeen produced and a period of years has elapsed,

---

[1] See 'NATO and the N+1 Problem' by Albert Wohlstetter, *Foreign Affairs*, April, 1961.

[2] A useful discussion of the whole problem of the spread of weapons with emphasis on this aspect is F. C. Ikle, 'Nth Countries and Disarmament', *Bulletin of Atomic Scientists*, December, 1960.

a secret stock becomes impossible to check and for every new nuclear power the permanent existence of one more force must be allowed for in a controlled or disarmed world.

Then finally, it is impossible to avoid the general conclusion that the addition of new powers to the list of those already equipped with weapons of mass destruction brings with it fear, uncertainty and a new incentive to military spending in neighbouring countries. Some areas like South America, Africa and the Middle East retain a distinctively non-nuclear character and it seems possible to say this of Asia as long as China has not obtained these weapons.

The spread, then, is undesirable and dangerous. It is also irreversible; once a country has reliable and tested nuclear weapons it has a potentiality which no renunciation can entirely remove. What can be done to limit it? The fact that it is taking place much more slowly than is generally assumed offers opportunities for measures which over a period of years might discourage it. In disarmament discussions it has now become commonplace to say that this is a matter in which the United States and the Soviet Union find themselves in a natural community of interest. Certainly concern with the problem gave powerful support to the British and American entry into negotiations for the abolition of nuclear tests in 1958 and may also have influenced the Soviet Union. It has also been the main reason for the western proposal for a cessation of the production of fissile materials for weapons purposes (the so-called cut-off), for the bilateral and multilateral (IAEA) controls on nuclear sharing and for certain inhibitions on allied technical co-operation. These undoubtedly have had a discouraging effect.

One important issue for the future is the extent to which nuclear power programmes will yield an option on weapons grade fissile material for countries which are now non-nuclear. The present decade will see the bulk of the nations which are industrially middle powers passing from their present stage of small research reactors to power reactors with their military possibilities. It is important that the assistance which most of these powers will receive from the advanced nuclear powers should be subject to effective safeguards. The experience of the

International Atomic Energy Agency so far is unsatisfactory. Though this is an obvious and important vehicle for a unified approach to this question, the present experimental safeguard system suffers from the criticism that it is discriminatory, that it demands an oversight where there can be little danger, and from the fact that it does not yet apply to large reactors. The great criticism is that, so far, few countries have made use of the Agency's facilities. It must be seen along with the normal bilateral agreements of the advance powers: and from the point of view of an intending nuclear power the question must be asked whether reactors, fissile material and facilities for chemical separation can be obtained from some source or other. In this matter much will depend on what policy is adopted by France and the Soviet Union as opportunities for the export of power reactors open to them. India might also eventually emerge as a supplier of refined natural uranium without controls. Even assuming a Russian anxiety not to promote the uncontrolled spread of nuclear technology around the world, the great powers are only likely to get rid of the small-power resistance to the IAEA controls if they show themselves willing to accept them on their own soil. The Indian proposal that all diffusion and separation plants should be brought under international inspection should be given serious consideration, if only because it comes from one of the leaders of opposition to the Vienna system[1]. As these plants are almost exclusively, at present, in the major powers' possession, it would right the imbalance in inspection activity which is behind many of the charges of colonialism. Since it would mean that the present powers would have to stop using new fissile material for nuclear weapons, it would involve taking a major step towards disarmament. It would amount, in fact, to the cut-off. The Soviet Union has frequently made it clear that it does not want inspectors in its plants; but with the security of its present stockpile of fissile material behind it there might be a possibility of creating such a system.

A ban on nuclear tests would probably do much to dis-

[1] Made at the Conference on the IAEA Statute in New York, September 2th—October 26th, 1956, by Dr. H. J. Bhabha, leader of the Indian delegation.

courage the spread of weapons. This has always been the hope
associated with this particular arms control measure. The
Commonwealth Prime Ministers, for example, (several of
which lead potential nuclear powers) said after their 1961
meeting: 'Every effort should be made to secure rapid agreement to the permanent banning of nuclear weapons tests by
all nations and to arrangements for verifying the observance of
the agreement. Such an agreement is urgent, since otherwise
further countries may soon become nuclear powers, which
would increase the danger of war and further complicate the
problem of disarmament.'[1] From the start of the three power
conference for such a ban in 1958, it was generally assumed
that most countries would adhere to the treaty once it was
agreed by the three. Certainly such countries as Sweden and
India would have put their names to it. At least one, France
would not have. M. Moch, the French delegate to the 1957
disarmament conference in London, made the following statement to the session on August 21st: 'To accept an end to tests
apart from an end to production (of fissile material) amounts
to leaving the most powerful arms to accumulate without limit
in the arsenals of the three states alone and would create
between equal powers a difference of fact of which the long
term consequences would be serious.' When the French bomb
was officially on the way and the test ban looked likely, M.
Moch said much the same thing:[2]

> Let these powers agree to halt, under control, the produc-
> tion of fissionable materials for weapons purposes, to begin
> the conversion of the stockpiles, and to eliminate the vehicle
> for these explosives . . . in short, to renounce a mono-
> poly . . . and that very hour France will adopt the same
> measures.

Here again is a trace of the Indian argument over the Vienna
system. The weak point in the western effort to make international controls effective is their unwillingness to accept
something like the cut-off. Nevertheless, a ban on nuclear

[1] Communiqué, London, March 17th, 1961.
[2] To the United Nations Political Committee. See the *Manchester Guardian*, November 5th, 1959.

tests, being universal, would obviously make things more difficult for a new nuclear power. It is not impossible to use an untested weapon (the United States must have done so against Japan since it used two different types of bomb after only one test) and a determined nation—such as France or China— would no doubt defy the ban. Nevertheless, the noise would be very great in a world without tests and the political opposition proportionately increased. It would also mean that the many countries without a suitable testing ground would have difficulty in finding one elsewhere, as they might otherwise hope to do.

The present difficulty of reaching any agreements between East and West discourages other proposals specifically designed to prevent the spread of nuclear weapons. Nevertheless, the common interest might be served by extending either formal or tacit agreement about sharing in nuclear power pro-grammes to exports of possible means of delivery. As was seen in Chapter 3, the United States has made some effort to restrict the supply of certain components associated with the French *force de frappe* and serious consideration should be given to restrictions on delivery systems to countries unwilling to give an undertaking to restrict themselves to conventional warheads. Because we are now discussing a class of countries which cannot easily undertake large sophisticated pro-grammes, their ability to meet the cost in both men and money is going to depend to a large extent on what they are able to buy. Countries planning an independent force should be treated by all the powers on quite a different basis from those which have renounced nuclear weapons. Where applic-able, the rivals of such countries should be particularly generously supplied with defensive weapons. Thus the United States would be justified militarily in supplying Pakistan with a far larger and more advanced force of interceptors and surface-to-air guided weapons if India decided to go into nuclear weapons. It might also make increasing provision across the whole range of modern conventional weapons. Russia might do the same for Egypt and Iraq in the face of an Israeli bomb programme. Anyone familiar with the defence problems of countries such as India or Israel will know how inconvenient such a prospect would be. With many powers, the more substantial weapons of aid and trade policy would also be very effective. These could not be effectively employed in a world in which the development of nuclear weapons involved no suggestion that a country was in some way acting improperly; but the circumstances of the first French bomb test show the extent to which the nuclear test moratorium created just such an atmosphere. An effective system of Vienna controls, a nuclear test ban, and a cut-off—all of them within the reach of the great powers—would undoubtedly confirm the present anti-nuclear climate throughout the world. It would then be relatively simple to apply pressures of the kind mentioned on countries trying to defy the system. They would attract a wide measure of support. This depends, of course, on a continuing understanding on these questions between Moscow and Washington. All logic says this should exist; experience, unfortunately, teaches a harsher lesson. It is nevertheless worth the effort, and in the absence of agreement the Russians might play along with a Western sponsored system without admitting it.

The present system of American bilateral agreements for establishing nuclear weapons on the territory of allies is open to serious charges. The procedures by which the warheads are maintained under United States control are not public and these explosives could presumably pass under the control of the host nation through some sort of seizure, a false message or a secret decision by the President that he has decided to change his policy. Although it appears to have few serious consequences at present, it can certainly be argued that an enemy who fears that the transfer might have taken place must assume that it has. Since the host country has the delivery systems for the warheads, the warning period inevitably associated with the emergence of an independent nuclear power does not exist. The tendency to tighter arrangements in United States policy must be welcomed in this respect, but serious consideration should be given to the continuing need to base nuclear weapons in large numbers on foreign soil.

The fact that the spread of nuclear weapons is going to be a long process associated with the creation of major industrial powers is the most obvious conclusion of this study. But the more significant conclusion is that many nations approaching this stage appear to be vigorously non-nuclear or content for the present with buying an option. This is a hopeful and promising situation. It should be clearly understood, however, that there are no simple technical ways to stop the spread of these weapons. The problem cannot be isolated. The decision to produce nuclear weapons is a major political undertaking and depends in the end on the safety which the world provides for the middle powers. It should be the aim of all governments to maintain and extend the present situation in which many countries prefer holding an option to embarking on the uncertain cost and effort (with an uncertain increase in security) involved in an independent force. No single measure will accomplish this, but a serious effort by the community of nations, led by the United States and Russia, to create the conditions in which a nuclear weapons programme will make a country an outsider in the world community can be expected to keep the number of nuclear powers manageably small for the foreseeable future. Indeed, if the present tendencies to unity in the west accelerate, the number may well decrease. There is no justification for a mood of resignation born of the impression that nuclear weapons are spreading as inevitably and surely as electric power or any other symbol of modern industrialism. There is nothing inevitable about them.

Index

Date Due